4

U

Look for other *SHOW STRIDES* books:

#1 School Horses and Show Ponies

#2 Confidence Comeback

#3 Moving Up and Moving On

4

· SHOW STRIDES ·

Testing Friendships

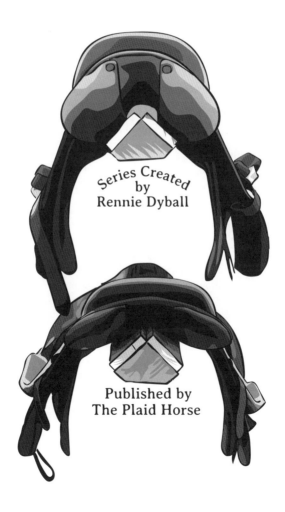

Series Created
by
Rennie Dyball

Published by
The Plaid Horse

Library of Congress Control Number: 2021913947
Show Strides: Testing Friendships / Piper Klemm
Text by Rennie Dyball
Illustrations © 2021 by The Plaid Horse

ISBN: 978-1-7329632-3-8

Printed in the United States of America
First Printing

Silver Lake Press
www.silverlakepress.net / 781-293-2276

MAP OF
QUINCE OAKS

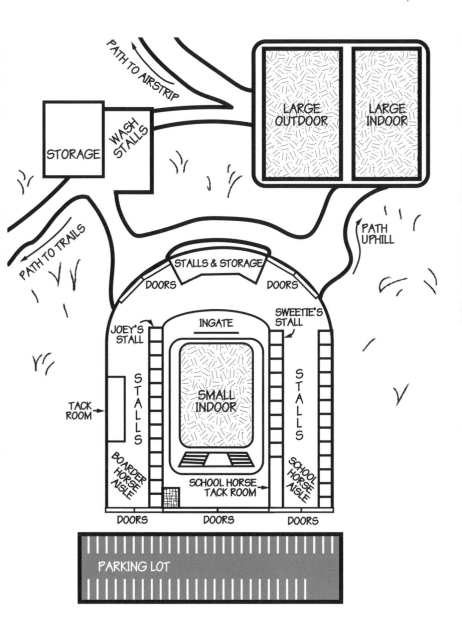

CHAPTER 1

"Change direction!"

Ryan's voice boomed through the large indoor ring as Tally Hart guided Sweetie, her favorite school horse, on a half turn to start tracking left. She wondered if Ryan's voice got hoarse by the end of the day.

"Tally, just pulling on your inside rein and having your horse respond by turning is not enough," Ryan said. "Every time you make a turn, you need to be thinking about *shaping* that turn. Don't just let her fall in."

It always seemed to happen this way. The minute Tally's mind wandered in a lesson, Ryan noticed and snapped her right back into reality. There was no room for thinking about anything except what was going on beneath her. And right now, making the transition back to Sweetie was demanding all of her attention.

After months of riding Ryan's sale pony Goose, Tally felt challenged by the little school horse in an entirely different way. Goose was green and game for anything. Sweetie had been there and done that—with dozens of kids in the lesson program—and wasn't inclined to shape a turn unless her rider politely insisted upon it.

"Let's do a couple of downward transitions," Ryan called out. "Tally and Maggie, think about keeping your leg on so that your horses don't fall into the walk on their front ends. Mac, you work on asking for the walk with soft hands, just sinking in and squeezing your reins."

Tally visualized her walk transition before she asked Sweetie to do it. She closed her leg first before closing her fingers. When Sweetie took hold of the bit and tried to just keep trotting, Tally bent her elbows and set herself down into her saddle.

"Whoa," she said softly to the mare, who slowed to a collected trot and then a walk. Tally was careful to relax her arms and hands the moment that Sweetie listened.

"Good, Tally. Did you feel how she stayed engaged in her hind end there and didn't just slow down by falling on to her front end?" Ryan asked. "Not bad for you either, Maggie, but next time, even a little more leg, okay? Lil is always happy to slow down, so it's going to take a lot from you to get a quality walk out of a pony like that. Mac, way to finesse it there with your aids, keeping everything soft. Everybody walk a lap and then we'll canter."

After the lesson wrapped up and Tally cooled out Sweetie, she walked from the school aisle to the boarder aisle to find Mac (short for Mackenzie) Bennett, her best friend from riding. Their barn, Quince Oaks, was shaped like a horse-shoe, home to a large lesson program on one side, and a group of boarders—most of whom showed on the A Circuit—on the other.

Tally's trainer, Ryan McNeil, taught lessons for the riding school in addition to running his own show business, Field Ridge, for the boarding clients. Since Ryan arrived at Oaks last year, he'd seen promise in Tally and had been giving her catch rides on sales ponies. Goose, the green pony she'd helped bring along at home and at the shows, was sold just a week ago at Pony Finals in Kentucky.

A warm breeze drifted down the boarder aisle from the open end of the barn. In the winter, there were massive doors to close off the aisle and keep the horses warm inside. Tally wished it could stay summertime forever. She bent down to retrieve her weathered Oaks baseball cap from inside her grooming box and threaded her long brown ponytail through the hole in the back.

"Tal! Come look at this."

Tally peeked inside the Field Ridge tack room to find Mac standing in front of the photo collage on the wall.

"What is it?"

"I don't know who took this picture, but look how gorgeous it turned out," Mac said, pointing to a newly-placed photo of a dapple-gray pony jumping an oxer with birch rails. Tally squinted at the photo, trying to place the pony and the rider, who had a calm but steely look on her face as she guided the fancy pony over the jump.

"Wait...is that *me*?"

Mac shot her a confused glance and laughed. "Uh, yeah, who did you think it was?"

"I actually didn't recognize either of us at first! Wow, look at how great Goose looks. That was such a fun day." Tally thought back to her ticketed schooling rounds at the Kentucky Horse Park with the pony. Sometimes it almost felt like a dream: In the space of a year, she'd gone from riding lesson horses and only showing at her barn's schooling series to competing at several A-rated shows, plus schooling and spectating at Pony Finals and Devon.

Gazing at the photo, Tally took in Goose's sweet expression, his perfect squared knees, his round topline. It had been incredibly hard to say goodbye to him, and she continued to feel an ache at seeing his empty stall at home. Still, she was happy that he now had a person of his very own. And before they left Kentucky, Ryan mentioned a potential new project horse that she might be riding next. Tally took one last look at the photo collage before leaving the tack room. It felt like she was officially part of the team at Field Ridge.

U

The next day, Tally was working a morning shift on the school aisle. The Oaks barn manager, Brenna, had given her an unofficial working student position—in exchange for each shift she worked caring for the school horses, she earned an extra riding lesson.

In the summer, Tally liked starting her shifts early to make herself available to Ryan by lunchtime. He'd come to depend on her to flat horses that weren't getting training rides or being ridden by their owners on a given day. Sometimes that meant no riding, but other times it meant flatting one or even multiple horses or ponies.

"Morning, Lil." Tally greeted each schoolie as she filled their water buckets. Her first task of the morning was watering the school aisle—at last count, Oaks had twenty-seven school horses and ponies, so it wasn't a quick job. While she filled a nearly-empty bucket in the stall near the riding school bulletin board, Tally scanned a flyer about the next Oaks schooling show in September. It would be the first weekend after she'd be back at school. Tally calculated how much summer she had left. There were about three more weeks in which barn time could be her top priority. School would take over that spot soon.

"Hey, Tal, after the hay and water are done, could you choose a horse or two to cross off the bathing list, please?"

Tally turned to answer Brenna, who was fiddling with a fan on a stall across the aisle.

"Sure, no problem."

"Thanks. And I was just looking at the birthday calendar in the office upstairs. I can't believe you're about to be 13, Tally! Way to make the rest of us feel old. How long have you been riding here now?"

Tally smiled. "I started in second grade. I was so little that Meg had to wrap my stirrup leathers," she said, remembering her first riding lessons at Oaks. She continued riding with Meg for years until her instructor took a job with a college equestrian team.

"And now Ryan says you need to *stop* growing so you can keep riding the ponies," Brenna said with a smile. "You've come a long way, Tal. I'm really proud of you, kiddo."

Once all the school horses had been watered, Tally distributed a flake of hay to each stall that was running low, and then checked the bathing list. Sweetie was still on it, so Tally crossed the mare's name off and brought her outside to the wash stalls.

After spraying down the little mare, a chestnut Thoroughbred cross, Tally squatted down beside her and scrubbed antifungal soap into the mare's legs where horses were prone

‿

to rain rot. She glanced up at Sweetie, whose ears had settled between a peeved expression and one of indifference.

"You know, if you dropped the grumpy act for a minute, you might actually enjoy this," Tally said to her. Sweetie flicked an ear in her direction.

Tally took her time finishing Sweetie's bath and then bathed another school horse named Cosmo. People always complained about keeping gray horses clean, but Tally loved the instant gratification of taking a visibly stained and muddy horse and returning them to their natural color. It also made her think of Goose. She wondered when his dark dapple-gray coat would start to turn white like Cosmo's. All gray horses' coats changed that way as they aged.

Tally used a sweat scraper to pull the excess water from Cosmo's coat, then led the gelding over to a patch of grass to continue drying in the sun. She looked up the hill to the entryway of the indoor. A couple of the boarders were filing out atop their horses, and Ryan walked out behind them.

"Have time to ride one?" Ryan asked Tally as he made his way down the hill.

"As soon as this guy's legs are dry," Tally answered. It was still a thrill every time she was asked to ride.

"Great. I have a lesson at one, so bring Beau up to the outdoor ring then, all right? I want to watch him go and make sure he looks sound."

"Thanks, Ryan," said Tally. "See you then!"

CHAPTER 3

Beau was a big-bodied, large bay pony with two white socks and a snip. He was adorable to look at, and had a personality to match. Tally got him ready on the cross ties behind Mac, who had her own medium pony, Joey, on the next set of cross ties.

"My mom bought the video of my round at Pony Finals," Mac told Tally as she pulled Joey's half pad up under the pommel of her saddle.

Tally smiled, recalling her friend's nearly flawless trip around the enormous Walnut ring at the Kentucky Horse Park, culminating in an uncharacteristic rail at the very last jump. Tally was so impressed by Mac's ability to laugh it off and appreciate all the good that came from her round, rather than focus on the mistake at the end.

"Ryan watched the video too, and he thinks I came back with my body a little early, which could be why Joey hit the back rail with his hind foot," Mac continued, pulling her blond hair down over her ears and securing it in a low ponytail. "Plus, Joey had to be a little tired by then. That ring is like a football field!"

"It didn't look like you came back early," Tally told her, buckling the throat latch on Beau's bridle.

"I don't remember doing it either, but Ryan says it can happen at the end of your trip, or when you're excited—and I was definitely excited that we got around that course." Mac rubbed Joey's neck and he turned to face her.

"No treats right now, buddy," she told him, scratching his forehead. "Workout first!"

The girls walked their ponies out of the boarder aisle and up the hill toward the outdoor ring, situated just outside the farm's large indoor. Before Tally started going to horse shows off the property, she didn't realize how lucky they were to have *two* indoor rings and a large outdoor ring. Plenty of riding facilities didn't even have one indoor to use during the winter months or when it was raining.

Ryan was sitting on a jump in the center of the outdoor ring when Tally and Mac arrived with the ponies. He explained to Tally that Beau had been a little off in his right hind for about a week—likely the result of too much fun in turnout with his buddies. The vet didn't suspect it was anything serious, and she recommended that Ryan watch the pony under saddle every couple of days and note the pony's progress.

"Take a nice long time walking around the ring, Tally," Ryan said. "A full lap on a loose rein and then you can pick up some contact, okay? Walk around the jumps, make some circles, and get him moving off your leg and bending. But just at the walk. He's been standing in his stall since all the horses came in this morning, so I want him really warm and loose before we trot."

Tally double-checked Beau's girth, mounted up, and walked toward the long side of the ring on top of the hill, overlooking the paddocks. She glanced down at the empty turnout fields in the valley below and up the hill in the distance. She smiled as Beau let out a big breath. Tally loved when horses and ponies did that—a sign that they were feeling relaxed and content.

Behind her, Tally heard Mac and Ryan talking about where they would show next, once Joey had another week or two off after Kentucky. As Tally and Beau completed their lap on a loose rein, Tally changed direction and began to slowly gather up her reins. Mac was standing atop the mounting block and Joey looked like his usual sweet self, almost half asleep since he hadn't started to work yet. Mac put her left foot into the stirrup and Joey stepped away from the mounting block.

That's when they heard the crash.

Glancing over her shoulder, Tally could see that a truck had smashed through the fencing around the turnout fields, noisily snapping and splitting the wood.

The ponies heard it, too.

Tally felt Beau shoot forward underneath her, away from the sound of the crash. And out of the corner of her eye, she watched Joey leap sideways. Mac, with only her left foot in the stirrup, never had a chance to swing her right leg over. She hit the ground hard as Joey raced for the gate.

· CHAPTER 4 ·

"Whoa...*whoa*...easy, ponies..."

Ryan's voice was calm but he was walking fast toward Mac, who hadn't moved from the spot where she landed. Beau had calmed down fairly quickly from his reaction to the noise. Now he was just prancing a bit, his head high and his ears trained hard in the direction of the paddocks. Joey was loose in the ring.

"Easy, Beau, easy," Tally said softly. She squeezed her fingers around the reins and forced herself to take a deep breath. She turned Beau away from the road, brought him down to a walk and then halted. She hopped off him quickly, rolled up her stirrups, and loosened the girth a couple of holes. Then she walked Beau toward the middle of the ring.

"I think it's her wrist," Tally heard Ryan saying into his phone. She was relieved to see that Mac was sitting up now, but her friend's face was red and streaked with tears. Tally felt a lump in her throat.

"Tally, stand here with Mac for just a minute, I'm going to grab Joey," Ryan instructed her. He strode confidently over to Joey, who, after racing around the ring, now stood by the gate, breathing hard and looking a little confused. Tally glanced down at Mac, who was gingerly holding her left wrist in her right palm.

"Walk both ponies down to the small indoor, Tal. I told Brenna you're coming," Ryan said, handing her Joey's reins. "Someone will be down there to help. They should both hand-walk a few laps before going back to their stalls after tearing around like that."

Tally nodded and positioned herself between the two ponies to lead them both down the hill, trying to hold back her own tears at the sight of her friend in pain.

Isabelle, one of Ryan's junior riders, was waiting at the bottom of the hill, and as Tally approached, she stretched a hand out toward Joey.

"Brenna asked me to come help. What happened?" she asked, her eyes wide. Tally handed her Joey's reins.

"A truck crashed into the fencing up the hill from the ring—out by the far paddocks. It spooked both of the ponies," Tally said, leading Beau to the smaller indoor ring between the two barn aisles.

Isabelle draped her arm over Joey's neck. "That's awful," she said. "What were you guys doing when it happened?"

"I was just walking Beau, and Mac was getting on Joey. I don't think she made it fully into the saddle. When Joey took off, she had no way of staying on. I think she really hurt her wrist."

"That's awful," Isabelle repeated, shaking her head. "Ryan

♘

wants us to hand walk these guys?"

"Yes. Oh shoot, I hadn't even trotted Beau yet and we were working him really slowly to check for soundness. He was fully cantering before I could pull him up. Do you think he looks okay?"

"Walk ahead of me," Isabelle said, watching the pony move. "Now turn across the middle of the ring...I think he looks fine. Don't worry about it though, Tally, it's not your fault. There's no way anyone can prevent a spook like that. If a horse hears a loud crash, he's going to run in the opposite direction. It's just how they're wired."

Tally and Isabelle hand-walked the ponies in silence, a couple of laps in one direction and then another couple of laps in the other. Each time Tally glanced up at the office, which overlooked the lower indoor, more and more people had gathered inside. Brenna had probably paused lessons in all the rings in the aftermath of the accident. Outside of the barn, a siren wailed. Joey and Beau both perked up at the sound.

"Shhh," Isabelle said to Joey, patting his neck. "He feels cool to me. I'll untack him if you can take care of Beau?"

"Of course," Tally replied, running her hand down Beau's chest. It was warm, but nothing out of the ordinary for a summer day.

Tally listened to the sounds of more sirens as she untacked Beau. She hoped the spook wouldn't set back his soundness, and she was really worried about her friend.

☙

On her way to grab a washcloth for the pony's coat, Tally spotted Mac's open backpack and trunk in the Field Ridge tack room. She zipped and closed up her friend's belongings, rinsed off Beau's bit, and walked back out to the pony on the cross ties to dry the sweat marks from his girth area. He turned toward her and Tally gave his forehead a quick scratch.

"You're okay, buddy," Tally said, rubbing the towel over his coat. "Hopefully Mac will be okay, too."

· CHAPTER 5 ·

Once she was finished with Beau, Tally walked outside and found Ryan making his way down the hill.

"Hey, Tal, thanks for taking the ponies."

"No problem," she said. "How's Mac?"

"She just left in an ambulance. You can never be too careful when it comes to concussions, so I want her to get checked out. I think she's okay though. Looks like a broken wrist for sure, but hopefully nothing more than that," he said. "Don't worry, Tal, she'll be fine."

"Okay," Tally said, certain that she wouldn't be able to keep from crying if she said another word.

"Let's jog Beau real quick, all right? Did he feel sound while he was careening across the ring with you?" Ryan asked with a dry little laugh.

"I honestly don't remember."

"That's fair." Ryan nodded. "I'll meet you in the small indoor."

Tally put a halter back on Beau, who wasn't super keen on leaving the hay in his stall since he'd thought he was done working for the day.

"Go ahead and jog alongside him so he'll trot," Ryan said when they got to the ring. Tally felt the lead rope pull tight behind her as she began jogging ahead of Beau. She glanced back at the pony, who looked like he wanted to go back to his stall for a nap.

"Don't look back at him, just keep jogging," called Ryan. Within a few more steps, the lead went slack and Beau was trotting next to Tally.

"Good, now just come halfway down the long side," said Ryan, and Tally was reminded of the times that Mac had to jog Joey at the shows. It wasn't as easy as it looked!

"Okay, that's good," Ryan said, and Tally slowed to a walk. Beau walked beside her. "He looks just fine to me. Let's try him under saddle again the next time you're here."

Tally felt a wave of relief and let out a big sigh. Isabelle was right—it wasn't her fault that Beau had taken off—but it was still reassuring to know that the pony was okay.

More news about the accident poured in over the next couple of hours. The driver of the truck was unhurt, but the fencing along the road would require extensive repairs. Mac had bruised her ribs and fractured her wrist. She would be in a cast for a minimum of four weeks. She didn't have a concussion, thankfully, so she was already home from the hospital.

The rest of Tally's afternoon at the barn was kind of a blur. When her mom picked her up, Tally filled her in on the day's events.

"Oh, Tally, that's really scary," her mom said, shaking her head as they pulled out of the parking lot. "It's easy to forget sometimes how unpredictable these animals can be."

As they followed the hilly road alongside the paddocks, Tally was able to check out the damage up close. The truck had destroyed a long stretch of fencing. Tally wondered how they would rearrange the turnout groups now that the farm was down one full paddock.

"Should we stop by Mac's? Is she home?" Tally's mom asked, interrupting her thoughts.

"Ryan said she's home, yeah."

Tally's mom tapped on the screen next to the driver's seat to make a call. Mac's mom picked up the phone.

"Cindy, hi, it's Stacy. I'm just leaving the barn with Tal. Is Mac up for visitors?"

A half hour later, armed with smoothies from the new juice shop up the road from the barn, Tally and her mom walked into Mac's house.

"She's up in her room, honey," Mac's mom told Tally, who took the stairs two at a time.

In her room, Mac was propped up on three pillows, with a fourth on her lap and her laptop balanced on top of that.

"Brought you a smoothie," Tally said, feeling awkward all of a sudden.

"Thanks," Mac replied, using her good hand to push herself up to sitting. Her wrist was wrapped in a hot pink cast and peeked out from inside a sling. She shut her laptop and tossed it toward the foot of her bed. "Ryan said Joey is okay. Did you see him?"

"Oh yeah, Joey's fine," said Tally, pulling Mac's desk chair next to the bed. She took a sip of her own smoothie. "Once we were back down at the barn I think he'd forgotten everything."

"He's such a good boy," Mac said, looking down at her arm in the sling. "I can't believe I'm stuck in this thing for a month," she added, scrunching her face up as she shifted positions.

"Does it hurt?" Tally asked.

"Yeah. And I bruised my ribs—that hurts even worse. My mom is pretty freaked out about this whole thing," added Mac. "She wants to wrap me in Bubble Wrap when I get back on. I really hope she's kidding."

Tally giggled. "My mom was talking about how unpredictable horses are when we were driving over here, so I might be getting Bubble-Wrapped, too. I don't even want to know what they are planning down there," she said, nodding toward the stairs outside Mac's bedroom door. "But that crash would have spooked any horse."

"What did Beau do? I didn't see anything but the dirt."

"The sound came from behind us," Tally said, "so he just made this big leap forward and then kinda turned into a racehorse on me."

"Don't make me laugh!" Mac groaned, holding her side. "Beau is, like, the laziest pony I've ever met. He must have really been scared."

"Tally!" her mother called from downstairs. "Ten minutes, okay? We should let Mac rest."

The girls both rolled their eyes.

"I've been home for one afternoon and I'm already running out of stuff to watch," Mac said.

"You mean you've watched *all* the big eq finals online?"

"I think I might have," said Mac. "But maybe I can find some hunter classes to watch from Indoors where they announce the scores. I'll play judge and see if I'm close."

"That actually sounds fun."

"Yeah, so much better than being at the barn," Mac said sarcastically. "Hey, will you ride Joey for me while I'm out?"

"I'd love to," Tally said. She'd always thought he looked like so much fun. "But I have to wait and see who Ryan asks me to ride each day."

"I know," said Mac. "But I'd feel better knowing you were riding him and loving on him."

Tally smiled. She enjoyed taking care of the horses and ponies almost as much as riding them.

"Oh, don't worry, I'll spoil him for sure. And I'll let you know as soon as I hear who's riding your boy."

· CHAPTER 6 ·

After an unusual four days off from riding (doctor's appointments and back-to-school shopping one day, followed by a long weekend at the beach with her cousins), Tally couldn't wait to get back to Quince Oaks.

"Bye, Mom, thanks for the ride," she said, opening the door while the car was still rolling up to the barn entrance.

"Slow down, Tal," her mom said with a laugh. "And be careful today, all right?"

"I'm careful every day."

"I know, but after what happened with Mac...it's just gotten me thinking about this sport and doing everything we can to keep you safe," her mom said. "I want to talk more with you, okay?"

"Fine. I mean, yes, sorry, we'll talk. Don't worry, Mom, I'm really careful."

Tally breezed down the boarder aisle, greeting the horses and ponies with their heads out before dropping her backpack on top of her tack trunk. She would work a shift for Brenna later in the day, and planned on grooming and riding whichever horses Ryan asked her to do first.

Tally stepped out into the aisle with a horse cookie for Joey. The nameplate on his stall always made her smile. He had such a fancy show name, Smoke Hill Jet Set, which didn't really match the sweet, goofy pony he was at the barn. The name definitely fit him in the show ring, though. Both he and Mac transformed when they picked up their canter on the way to the first jump. All business and polish.

"Hi, Tally," someone said from the back of Joey's stall.

"Oh, Maggie, hey," Tally replied. Maggie Edwards, a Black equestrian who was in eighth grade, also used to take lessons with Meg before Ryan joined the barn. Like Tally, she was close to outgrowing the small ponies at the barn but still fit on the mediums.

"Are you riding at nine with me?" Maggie asked as she led Joey out of his stall.

"I don't know yet, I have to go talk to Ryan," said Tally. "You're riding Joey while Mac is out?"

"I'm actually trying him today," Maggie said with a smile as she situated the pony between the cross ties. "I'm hopefully going to do a short-term lease with Joey. Ryan said it's to get me used to ponies like this before we shop for a pony for me."

Tally knew she should be happy for Maggie—and part of her was—but she couldn't help feeling jealous that she didn't get to ride Joey herself. Or go shopping for a pony of her own, for that matter.

"That's awesome," Tally said, forcing a friendly smile. "He looks like a lot of fun."

"Have you ridden him? I'm so nervous, I don't know what to expect," said Maggie, bending down to pick out his right front hoof. That's when Tally noticed that Joey was in his leather show halter. It wasn't long ago that she had to learn the ins and outs of the boarder aisle herself.

"Hey, you're fine for today, but just use his regular break-away halter when you're grooming him. The leather halter is only for shows," Tally said kindly. She didn't want to embarrass Maggie.

"Oh my gosh," Maggie said, popping up and looking at the halter. Joey turned to look at her, as if wondering what all the fuss was about. "I'm like, clueless here, thank you so much."

"No, no, you're fine," Tally quickly added. "There's just different ways of doing things with these horses than the school horses. I had to learn it all, too. Anyway, I haven't ridden Joey before, but Mac says he *loves* the jumps. Like, too much sometimes, and she usually has to whoa down the lines. He's got a perfect lead change, too. And he's just so sweet on the ground."

"I noticed that," Maggie said, grinning and looking more relaxed. "Thanks, Tally. I can't believe I'm actually going to be horse shopping! Ryan thinks Joey will give me a feel for what we're looking for. We're going to start looking later in the fall so the timing worked out to start with a short-term lease on Joey."

Up in the outdoor ring, Ryan was setting jumps while Isabelle and another boarder hacked around.

"Tally, hi. Let's see Beau trot around today, okay? Same as the other day, get him warm and loose at the walk first. And that new project horse arrived, so we'll do him after that," Ryan said.

Two rides for the morning—and one of them was the new horse Ryan mentioned! Tally felt a little guilty about being jealous of Maggie and reminded herself that she was lucky to be a catch rider for Ryan. It would be good for Joey, too, to have just one dedicated person while Mac was recovering.

Tally thanked Ryan and made her way back down to the barn to get Beau ready. She methodically groomed and tacked him for his hack and walked him back up the hill and into the center of the outdoor ring. Tally glanced out toward the broken fencing before mounting up on Beau. Then she cut across the ring to walk beside Maggie, who was finishing up with Joey.

"How was he?"

"He's really fun! But you were right—so much *whoa* to the jumps," she added with a laugh. "Such a good boy though."

"That's great," Tally said. And she meant it. The girls walked another couple of laps on a loose rein, chatting as they went.

"Go ahead and pick up your trot, Tal," Ryan called from the center of the ring. Tally made a half circle away from Joey to track in the other direction and Beau flicked his ears back in response. He was enjoying the leisurely stroll with his buddy. Back on the rail, Tally squeezed the pony with both legs and he responded with a swish of his tail and a little crow hop.

"Someone's not ready to get back to having a job," Ryan said with a laugh. "Just keep moving forward, don't let him just bounce around in place."

Tally trotted Beau in both directions, making circles and bending when the pony wanted to hop and play.

"He's just fresh since he's been off for a bit," Ryan said. "Ask him to canter, but sit up and lift your eye when you do it."

Tally signaled Beau with her right leg and the pony burst into a bouncy left lead canter.

"Forward, forward, forward," Ryan said. "Make a circle and bend him, keep his brain working in addition to his body."

Beau settled into a medium canter and Tally thought about sitting up tall while staying light in the tack. Then they walked a lap and cantered to the right.

"He's definitely sound," Ryan said. "Let him walk a lap or two and then I'll meet you on the aisle in a bit. Hope you're ready for a new project."

♘

· CHAPTER 7 ·

Tally took her time putting Beau away. Then she brought her saddle out to the big wooden rack on the aisle. It was the best spot for cleaning tack. Listening to the sounds of horses happily munching their hay, Tally wiped down all the leather. Her parents had purchased the saddle from Isabelle—letting Tally work off the cost with babysitting. Seeing her own name on the cantle nameplate always made her smile. It was the first piece of tack she owned, and she was determined to take good care of it.

With a clean sponge, Tally applied a thin layer of conditioner on the saddle flaps and a bit on the seat. The saddle was much softer and more delicate than the school saddles, so it took more work to keep it looking its best.

One of the adult boarders who owned a big gray gelding gave Tally a smile and a wave as she walked into the tack room. On the other side of the aisle, Tally could hear one of the riding school instructors calling out directions from the small indoor. Busy summer days at the barn were the best.

Tally ran her stirrups back up on her saddle and considered cleaning some of the pony bridles that looked a bit neglected when Ryan joined her on the aisle.

"Can I clone you, Tally?"

"What do you mean?" she asked with a laugh.

"I mean you actually *enjoy* cleaning tack, so you do it more than most," Ryan said. "We can never have enough tack cleaning." He gestured for Tally to follow him down to the far end of the aisle by the barn entrance.

"He's in this stall for now. Seems really social so he might like all the activity at the end here," Ryan said, stopping at the last stall on the aisle. "This one probably isn't like anything you've ridden before. He belongs to a friend of mine—he's her homebred. She ended up with a bigger herd than she intended, so he got leased by a big lesson program like ours, but it wasn't the right fit for him."

As if on cue, a small black horse with a white star walked up to the doorway and stretched his head out toward them.

"Hi, buddy," Ryan said, rubbing the little horse's forehead. "He's a Hanoverian cross, about 15 hands, so he might be a good fit for a kid coming off a pony."

Tally had learned that buyers generally wanted animals on the taller end of the ranges, since that usually meant the horse or pony would have a bigger stride. And you needed a big stride to get down the lines at the horse shows. Small ponies maxed out at 12.2 hands, so buyers usually wanted a small as close to that measurement as possible. Mediums went up to 13.2, larges went up to 14.2, and the smallest horses started at 14.3. So a horse that stood 15.1 hands was on the small side. Plenty of people only looked at horses who were 16 hands and up.

"Why didn't the lesson program work out for him?" Tally asked.

"His owner said they used him in at least one lesson a day, five or six days a week. It was a lot for him, having so many riders—he seems like the type that does best with his own person. A lot of the kids were beginners, too, so they were a bit rough on his mouth."

"What did he do?" Tally asked.

"Well, that's the interesting part. It turns out he's a sensitive guy with a good, soft mouth, so teaching kids with uneducated hands wasn't the right job for him. But he never did anything really bad. No bucking, no stopping at the jumps. Just some kicking out when he's asked to canter, which everybody chalked up to him being unhappy or maybe a little sore. My friend Lara, who owns him, said he doesn't even pin his ears."

Tally smiled at the horse, who stood calmly studying her and Ryan. He had a beautiful face and a nearly symmetrical star. He reminded her of Black Beauty.

"What's his name?"

"Obie. I rode him the other day when he got here and he's super quiet. Lara brought him home from that lesson program, but between work and having young kids, she hasn't been able to ride. He's been turned out for the summer since June," said Ryan. "It'll be a process to get him into shape and to be less defensive about his mouth. Can you bring him up in an hour or so?"

"Sounds good," Tally said.

"Great. There's an old trunk in the tack room with all his stuff in it. I'll get a bridle rack up for him this week. See you soon."

CHAPTER 8

When Tally was little, her parents had a cat named Frankie who liked to watch everything Tally did. And when he was in the mood, he'd rub his head on her leg and relish whatever pets and cuddles she'd give him. Obie immediately reminded her of that cat.

All three sets of cross ties were occupied, so Tally got started grooming Obie in his stall. As she worked some mud out of his right front hoof with her hoof pick, Obie rested his chin gently on her back. Instantly, Tally was reminded of Goose doing the same thing. It had startled her the first time he did it, but with Obie it felt like a sweet, familiar gesture. She took her time picking out Obie's right front hoof, enjoying the closeness of the horse's company.

Not knowing whether this new horse would enjoy a good curry, Tally selected her softer grooming gloves and went over Obie's coat slowly to start. He barely blinked as she did, so she applied more pressure and he turned to watch her again. There was something so kind and gentle in his expression.

After a once-over with both her stiff and soft brushes, Tally closed and latched Obie's stall door. He lifted his head and neck over the door to continue watching her. In the tack room, Tally opened the corner tack trunk, marked with a cursive *L* on the nameplate, and found a bridle, square saddle pad, size 48 girth, and a fuzzy half pad. She fished around to see if there was a martingale, or boots, or anything else the horse might wear to be ridden, but she came up empty. There were two folded blankets at the bottom of the trunk, plus an old leather halter. Tally ran her finger along the side, already thinking about how much she wanted to condition the leather to soften it up. The nameplate read "Oceanfront."

Back at Obie's stall, Tally fastened the harness on her helmet—a trick she learned back in the days of summer horse camp. The instructor told them to always fasten their harness *before* tacking up. That way, they could be sure they wouldn't forget to do it by the time they were mounted.

Tally placed the square pad on Obie's back, the half pad on top of that, and started to lift her saddle off her hip when Ryan walked by Obie's stall.

"Tally, *what* are you doing?" he nearly shouted.

Tally froze. "Tacking up?" she said, her voice barely above a whisper.

"That horse is loose in his stall without even a halter on. You don't know him at all, Tally. You never, *ever*, put the saddle on first with a loose horse—you have no way of controlling him if something went wrong. What if he spooked? Or tried to kick? What would you do?"

Tally placed her saddle in the corner of the stall and looked down at her feet. She hadn't even thought about whether to put the saddle or the bridle on first.

"Why are you tacking up in the stall, anyway?"

"All three cross ties were full when I was grooming him. I guess I'm just so used to doing the saddle first when the horses are on the cross ties that I...did it here, too," Tally said.

"That's muscle memory. But you can't get complacent around horses. You have to think, each and every time, about how you're going to go about these things. See this?" Ryan pointed at the metal ring on the stall wall. "The whole point of having one of these in the stall is so that you can tie up your horse while you handle him in the stall. Do you know how to tie a quick-release knot?"

Tally nodded, the tears in her eyes threatening to spill over.

"Look, I'm being hard on you because this is so important," Ryan said. "I need to review all kinds of safety precautions with you guys. You can never take anything for granted with horses and you always have to be thinking about what could go wrong and position yourself accordingly. Okay?"

Tally nodded again, quickly swiping under her eyes.

"If you don't tie him in his stall, at least put the bridle on first. Then you have the reins over the neck to control him if things go sideways while saddling. Got it?"

"Got it," Tally said with a sniff. "Makes sense. I just didn't think it through."

"Last time that'll happen," Ryan replied with a hint of a smile. "I'm going to make all of my riders better horsemen and horsewomen with these safety lessons."

Up at the ring, Tally waited with Obie as a girl named Lauren got on Scout, one of the school horses. As Lauren swung her right leg up above the saddle, Scout took a step forward.

"Lauren, *halt*," Ryan said, using that same tone he'd used with Tally at Obie's stall. "What was wrong with that mount?"

Tally thought back on Mac's accident. *Didn't Joey do the same thing, walking off from the mounting block before Mac had gotten fully into the saddle?*

"I'm...not sure," Lauren answered, looking as shell-shocked by Ryan's reaction as Tally had felt down at the barn.

"Everyone walk your horses into the center," Ryan called out. The three horses and riders schooling in the outdoor ring walked over, joining Tally and Lauren.

"Things change starting *today* with the way we mount," he began. "Too many horses begin walking off before the rider is fully in the saddle. Everyone knows what happened to Mac a few days ago, right?"

All five riders nodded. Tally caught Isabelle's eye and they exchanged a knowing glance.

"That accident might have been prevented if Joey stood at the mounting block as a habit. But he walked off before Mac was in the saddle, just like this horse did, which put Mac in a precarious spot with no chance to stay on when he spooked."

Ryan stood next to Scout while Lauren dismounted and climbed up the mounting block once again. "I'll stand here for each of you until this becomes a habit for every horse in the barn. Go ahead and get on."

It took a couple tries before Scout stood calmly next to the block without Ryan holding his head, waiting until Lauren cued him to walk.

"You can stay light in your seat—don't sit down hard. But make him hold that halt until you've got both feet in your irons and you're ready to walk off. That's better, Lauren. Tally, you're up."

Tally followed Ryan's instructions and Obie watched Ryan closely.

"Good," Ryan said as Tally mounted a motionless Obie. She settled softly into the saddle. "*Now* you can walk out to the rail."

Tally squeezed his sides and Obie ambled off toward the long side. She squeezed again to get a more forward walk but nothing happened. Once on the rail, Tally tried thumping with her left leg and then her right—she'd read that it was a good way to get more animation out of a horse's walk. Nothing. *Well, this was new.*

"Tally, we're just going to do a little flatting today to get a feel for this one, okay? Walk around, go in between the jumps, and let him see the ring."

Tally steered Obie around all the jumps. He was as quiet as the school horses she'd ridden, so it made sense that he'd ended up in a lesson program. But his rubber snaffle told a different story. This horse had a soft, sensitive mouth.

"Go ahead and trot down the long side, Tal, let's see what we've got!"

Tally asked, asked again, then asked more firmly for Obie to trot. When he picked up the new gait, Tally was delighted at how floaty and smooth it felt—not at all bouncy.

"Not enough, let's get more impulsion," said Ryan. "Post softly…better. Ah-ha, he told on you there, didn't he?"

After just half a lap of posting trot, Obie had quickly down-shifted back to the walk without any input from Tally.

"Your shoulders got ahead of his shoulders, so he took that as an invitation to break. Don't use your upper body to keep him moving forward, use your *leg*. Try again."

Tally worked harder in the next fifteen minutes than she'd worked on her last few horses altogether. Obie was as sweet and kind as could be, but his preferred speed seemed to be about three miles per hour.

Ryan called Tally into the center of the ring and explained that when a horse had significant time off, as Obie had, they would lose a lot of their fitness. And fast. Obie would have to be eased slowly back into work.

"Let's get just a little canter out of him before we quit for today, Tal. He seemed to prefer the left lead when I rode him, so track left. You can ask from the trot if you want. Sit up tall, don't beg with your body."

Tally sat lightly as Obie trotted and then signaled him to pick up his left lead canter with her outside leg. Nothing. Holding herself upright, she upgraded her squeeze to a thump on his side. Still nothing.

"Sit up taller, you're asking with your shoulders again!" called Ryan.

Tally felt herself start to bounce around in the saddle. She slowed Obie to a walk to reorganize. Taking a deep breath, she asked for the trot and then the canter again.

"There! There! Hold that, stay light in your seat!"

Obie skipped across the ground, his canter as comfortable as his trot. Maybe even more comfortable. But they didn't make it very far. The second Tally relaxed her leg pressure, Obie was happy to break to the trot again.

"That's all right, Tal, let him walk," Ryan said. Tally wiped her face with the back of her glove. She was *covered* in sweat. She could feel Obie breathing hard underneath her.

"We'll get him back into shape one day at a time," Ryan said. "And in the meantime, you have to ask correctly or he won't give it to you. This horse is gonna fine-tune your aids, huh?"

Tally laughed to herself under her breath. *Sure, something like that.*

That night, she sat out on her deck overlooking the backyard while her mom grilled burgers and corn.

"James?" Tally's mom called to her dad. "Can you bring me the hamburger buns?"

Tally frowned in her seat as she watched a group of birds gather in the big pine tree at the back of their yard. It was very rare to have a bad day at the barn. It put her in a bad mood for the rest of the night.

Tally's dad opened the sliding door and handed Stacy a package of hamburger buns before sitting down in the chair next to his daughter.

"Why the long face?" he asked her.

Tally shrugged.

"You know you're not getting away with *that* as an answer," her dad said dryly.

"It was just a bad day. Ryan yelled at me and then I got on this new project horse who I couldn't even get to canter," said Tally. "I was so tired for my shift for Brenna that I let the wheelbarrow tip over and it took me forever to clean up. I couldn't do anything right today."

Her father gazed out over the backyard. "What did Ryan yell about?"

"I was just tacking up in the stall, it wasn't a big deal."

"Then why did he yell?"

Tally crossed her arms. "Because it was technically dangerous, I guess. To put the saddle on first without a halter or bridle on the horse."

Tally's dad was quiet.

"He's probably just worried after what happened to Mac," Tally continued. "He's looking for things to yell about."

"It sounds to me like he's looking to make everyone safer. Working with horses is all about habits, right? And if you can improve the habits that make you safer, you'll be better off, don't you think?"

⊍

Tally liked it better back when her dad didn't know anything about horses.

After dinner outside, Tally was in a slightly better mood. She called Mac, who was getting antsy about not being able to ride. Tally told her about struggling to canter on Obie.

"He's really that lazy?" Mac asked.

"Ryan says it's partly because he's out of shape. He's really sweet, though. I don't think he put his ears back once, even with me flopping and kicking up there trying to get him to canter."

Mac giggled. "I'm sure you weren't flopping. Hey, my mom is going to drop me off at the barn for like an hour on Friday to watch Maggie ride Joey. Will you be there?"

"Yes!" Tally said. "I'm so excited you're coming out."

"Me too. It feels like it's been a year. I'll see you then."

CHAPTER 9

That Friday morning, Tally and Mac both got dropped off at the barn a little before nine o'clock.

"You're back!" Tally said, racing from her car to Mac's. "Can I hug you? Gently?"

Mac nodded. "My ribs only hurt a little, and mostly at night now," she said as she hugged Tally back with her good arm. Her broken wrist was still positioned against her chest in a sling. "The itching inside the cast is the worst. Let's go watch the lessons. That'll distract me."

Gray clouds gathered overhead as the girls walked up the hill to the ring. Mac told Tally that Maggie's lesson started at nine, and she didn't want to be a distraction.

"I remember how nervous I was when I leased a pony and the owner came to watch," she said.

Mac seemed a little winded as the girls sat down on the bleachers in the big indoor ring, but she hadn't stopped smiling since arriving at the barn. Maggie was trotting Joey around while Ryan set some jumps. After adjusting a ground line at a vertical, he stood up and watched as Maggie circled around an oxer.

"The outside aids set the limit for how far he should bend," Ryan said to Maggie. "He's very willing to bend around your leg, but set the limit with your outside leg. Better. Keep him on a track between your legs and hands. Mac, hi!"

Ryan strode over to the bleachers with a big smile for Mac. "So glad to see you, Mac Attack. You really look none the worse for wear."

"Does that mean you'll let me ride before I get this stupid thing off?" Mac asked, waving the cast on her wrist.

"What do you think? You just keep healing and you'll be back on in no time. Your pony is in good hands. He's happy and fit. Be sure you're drinking a lot of milk and stuff, huh? Calcium makes strong bones, or at least that's what the commercials say," he added, turning back to face the ring.

Mac rolled her eyes in Tally's direction and smiled. "He's so cheesy."

Maggie was cantering now, Joey covering the ground with his big, straight-legged stride. Tally never got tired of watching the pony go.

"Good, Mags, now come around and catch this cross-rail here," Ryan said.

Maggie jumped the cross-rail off both leads, with Joey looking like his usual, cheerful self.

"Are you scared to get back on?" Tally asked Mac.

"Nah. How often do trucks crash into fencing outside of our ring? I think it was a freak accident," Mac said, pausing to take a deep breath. "Ryan talked to me about letting Joey walk off at the mounting block. It's a bad habit. If I made Joey stand, I probably would have been in the saddle when he took off, and then this never would have happened."

Tally nodded. "Ryan yelled at me yesterday for putting Obie's saddle on in his stall without a halter or a bridle to control him."

"Guess he's on a safety rampage now."

In the ring, Ryan told Maggie to jump a bending line in five strides going away from the gate, a single gate on the diagonal, and then a forward outside line in six.

"Remember how adjustable this pony is," he said as Maggie approached the jump in to the bending line. "Everything is set for horse show strides. Jump in and just continue."

Maggie and Joey jumped in to the bending and Joey took two big strides after landing.

"Whoa," Ryan said. Tally watched as Maggie sat up in the saddle and Joey tossed his head.

"Three, four, five, *good*, Mags! Don't worry about his head, you rode that right. We can't let him barrel down the lines like a freight train."

"She really rides well," Mac whispered as they watched Joey and Maggie hunt down the single gate.

"Now you've got plenty of canter, so jump in and keep your rhythm up the six," said Ryan.

Maggie found a chip in to the line.

"You went past the distance there because he's on his nose!" Ryan called out. "Move up for your six!"

Tally could see Joey react to Maggie closing her leg. The pony lifted his head, but opened up his canter to meet the out of the line just right.

"Good! That's the ride. We'll work on finessing it as we go. For only a few rides in, this is great, Mags. Cool him out and we'll quit with that for today."

Once Maggie was done, the three girls walked down the hill together, rain starting to come down as a light mist. Back down at the barn, they all gathered around Joey.

"How are you so perfect?" Mac asked, wrapping up her pony's neck in a hug. "I miss you!"

"He is such a good boy. Thanks for letting me do this mini-lease with him," said Maggie.

"Sure. You really ride him well," said Mac.

Maggie grinned and lifted the saddle off the pony's back.

"What are you looking for when you go horse shopping?" Tally asked. "Something Joey-sized? Or bigger?"

"My parents want me to get a horse so we can be, like, one-and-done on the shopping," Maggie said. "They don't want to do the whole buying and selling thing with a pony and then a horse. But I want to do the ponies for a few years while I can. If I don't do it now, I'll never be able to, you know? So, I guess we'll see what they decide."

It was not that long ago that Tally learned the rules of the regular pony hunter divisions herself. Small ponies could only be shown by riders who were twelve or younger. You could show mediums until you were fourteen, and any junior rider could show large ponies.

"What does Ryan think?" Mac asked.

"He hasn't really said anything about that. Just that he wants me to try everything with an open mind."

"Oh my gosh, I tried a lot of ponies that didn't work out for me before we found Joey," said Mac. "I fell off one pony twice in a trial. He kept wanting to take the winger as we were schooling around. Or maybe I did, I can't remember. I'm pretty sure my trainer wanted to kill me."

"You do love a long spot," Tally said with a laugh.

Maggie gestured toward the aisle doorway. "I'm going to take Joey out to the wash stall if you guys want to join me. Who are you riding now, Tally?" she asked.

"I'm riding Obie, the new project horse that Ryan brought in," Tally said, falling in step next to Maggie and Mac. "We're getting him back in shape after being turned out for a few months. He was a schoolie at another barn but it wasn't the right job for him. We're trying to figure out what would be a better fit."

"Tally, you are *so* cool," Maggie said as they reached the wash stalls.

"What do you mean?"

"She means you just get on anything and you ride them all so well," Mac said. Maggie nodded. "I want to ride like that," added Mac. Tally felt her face turn several shades of red. She'd admired Mac's riding since the day they met. It was one of the nicest compliments she'd ever received.

♘

· CHAPTER 10 ·

After Joey's bath, Tally and Mac came back to the barn and found Ryan in the tack room.

"The farrier is going to put shoes on our barefoot friend Obie this afternoon, so you'll ride him again tomorrow."

"Okay," said Tally.

"My mom actually just texted me," Mac chimed in. "She and your mom want to take us to the tack shop today."

"Perfect timing," Ryan said, winking at them both.

What was that about?

Tally and Mac stopped by Obie's stall on their way out of the barn, scratching his forehead and slipping him a couple of peppermints.

"It'll be fun to see how he goes as he gets into shape," Mac said. "It's kind of like unwrapping a present. You don't know what you've got yet."

"That's a good way to think about it," Tally said. It was still misting outside so she pulled her Oaks baseball cap onto her head. "I'm still sore from getting him to canter so I'll try to remember that present thing the next time my legs are about to fall off!"

In the car, Mac and Tally's moms were oddly quiet. It was almost impossible not to notice a weird vibe going on.

"What's up with you guys?" Mac asked.

"Well, we sort of planned something with Ryan," her mom said.

"Uh oh," groaned Tally.

"We want to make sure you guys are as safe as you can possibly be up on those horses," Tally's mom added. "So, we're going to the tack store to get you fitted for safety vests."

Tally and Mac looked at each other in the back seat. That must be why Ryan had been so weird about sending them off after Maggie's lesson.

"I called the store, and they said they can find a good fit for you without making the vest too tight," Mac's mom told her daughter.

The car went quiet again.

"I think they're thrilled by this idea," Tally's mom joked.

"It just seems like a bit much after a freak accident. How often do trucks crash into paddock fencing?" Tally said, echoing what Mac had wondered aloud earlier.

The moms glanced at each other, sharing a small, wordless conference. Tally and Mac did the same.

"I think that's the whole point of wearing a vest," Mac's mom began. "You never know when something might go awry. That's why you wear your helmet every single ride, right? Even if you were just walking, you wouldn't skip the step of putting on your helmet."

♆

"Hold on, do you mean you want us wearing vests for *every* ride?" Mac was wide-eyed now.

"Yes," her mom replied. "If there's an additional safety precaution that you can take, we want you to take it. Every time you ride."

They pulled into the tack shop parking lot a few minutes later. No one was happy. The moms wanted the girls to take safety more seriously, but neither Tally nor Mac was thrilled at the idea of adding on a new layer of riding clothes in the summer. Or ever.

"Wait, what about for horse shows?" Tally asked as everyone got out of the car. "A vest would cover up our show coats."

"Lucky for you, Ryan already discussed that with us," said her mom. "According to the rule book, vests are allowed in the show ring and you can't be penalized for wearing them. And, Ryan supports you two wearing them every ride."

A saleswoman—Sam, her name tag read—greeted the foursome inside the store. Tally's mom told her what they were looking for and Sam led them to a rack near the helmets.

Tally was relieved that Sam was helping them this time. On a shopping trip to the same tack store earlier that summer, another saleswoman had made a comment about the way Mac's body looked in show coats. It had been an upsetting experience for Mac, who started feeling insecure about her shorter, more muscular body as a result. Not long afterward, Isabelle had talked to them about what happened. Isabelle referred to herself as "more strong than skinny," Tally remembered. All three girls decided that being strong for their horses was most important, no matter what that meant about their body shape.

"Vests are becoming so much more acceptable in the hunter ring," Sam was telling the group. "And popular—we can hardly keep certain styles in stock."

Sam explained that the traditional body protectors, the type eventers wore, would provide protection to the ribs and vital organs in the event of a fall. The newer air vests (popular for their streamlined look, among other reasons) featured a lanyard that connected the vest to the saddle. The "air bag" would deploy if the lanyard detached in the event of a fall.

"Let's start by trying some on and seeing what fits well," said Sam. "And Mac, we won't strap you in too tight if your ribs are still hurting. You guys all know that you should always replace your helmet after a fall, even if you're not sure whether you hit your head?"

Everyone nodded.

"I'll do that while we're here, too," said Mac's mom.

It didn't take long for Tally and Mac to try on nearly every vest in the store. Both ended up with a body protector, while Mac also convinced her mom to get her an air vest to try as well. Tally's mom wanted her to get used to one vest first before buying a second.

"I still can't ride, so I guess you're the guinea pig," Mac said to Tally when they were all back in the car. "Let me know how it goes when you wear it tomorrow."

U

· CHAPTER 11 ·

The next day, when it came time to groom and tack Obie, the cross ties were all occupied again. Tally dutifully tied Obie's lead rope to the metal ring in his stall using a quick-release knot, smiling to herself when he gave her a confused-looking glance.

"I know you're not going anywhere, sweet boy," she said, stroking his neck. "But we're working on our safety habits so...here we are."

Once Obie was groomed and saddled, Tally put on her new vest in his stall. Sam had told them that the foam would flex and mold once it came into contact with body heat. Tally hoped Sam was right—the vest was so stiff at first she felt like the Tin Man from *The Wizard of Oz*.

By the time she walked Obie up to the outdoor ring, however, Tally begrudgingly acknowledged that the vest had already become much more comfortable.

"Definitely lots of body heat today," she whispered to Obie.

Once Tally was up in the saddle and walking around, the vest did, in fact, move with her. It didn't feel like a hindrance at all. But it was definitely hot.

"Looking good, Tally," Ryan called from the center of the ring, where he was helping a rider tighten their girth. "How does the vest feel?"

"Like I'm being cooked in a microwave."

Ryan let out a hearty laugh. "You'll adjust to that, I promise. One of my old clients moved to Florida and does the big jumpers in a vest like that one. Heat is a state of mind, Tally. Be sure you're drinking enough water and then it's just about adjusting to the new layer. Nothing more than mind over matter."

Ryan told her to start trotting Obie around while he finished up his previous lesson. Tally wasn't sure if Obie would be footsore after having shoes put on the day before, but he felt just the same. She'd recently read about the phrase "no hoof, no horse" in a book about horsemanship. She hoped, for Obie's sake, that he had good feet.

"Keep those shoulders back as you trot around," Ryan called to her. "Remember that he'll take any invitation to slow to a walk, so don't invite him to do that with your body."

Tally could feel sweat trickling down her back underneath her vest—luckily, regular walk breaks were key for a horse getting back into shape. After walking for a bit, Ryan handed Tally a dressage whip.

"If you need to back up your leg, just make a little flicking motion with your wrist," he said. "Have you used a dressage whip before?" Tally shook her head no. "Okay, so the end of your whip is going to land right there behind your leg when you use it. You don't need force behind it, it's just a flick," said Ryan, demonstrating the motion with his hand over hers.

It took a few tries, but Tally finally got Obie to pick up his left lead canter, and when she felt like he'd break to the trot despite her squeezing, she added a flick of the dressage whip. She felt him come up underneath her.

"That's it, Tal, great!" Ryan said. "He hasn't used his back like this for a long time, let him walk."

While Obie walked a couple of laps, Ryan lifted the gate from a jump set near the middle of the ring and put it down off to the side of the standard. Then he took the rails that had been set atop the gate and dropped one side of each to form an X.

"Pick up your trot and come pop up over this little cross-rail," Ryan said as he adjusted one of the jump cups. "He's willing and loves to jump, but he was lied to a whole lot by the kids learning to ride on him. He's defensive about getting popped in the mouth so grab a handful of mane. Think about nothing but keeping him straight with your leg on."

Tally came out of the turn toward the cross-rail and Obie perked up quite a bit. She'd read about horses like this, too. Some horses just didn't have a whole lot of energy for flat-work, but they loved to jump. Maybe Obie was that type?

"Did you notice how he fell in there? Circle and make it a better turn, Tal."

Tally refocused on how Obie was trotting underneath her. She made the turn again with some shape and thought about keeping Obie between both her legs and both her hands.

"Better! Keep your eye up, look out past the fence. There. Now keep your leg on and grab the mane."

Tally held her two-point for the last couple of trot steps to be sure she didn't get behind Obie's motion. She grabbed mane like Ryan suggested and smiled as she felt the round, lofty effort that the horse gave the little jump.

"Good! Canter away!"

Tally kept her leg on and got several canter steps out of Obie.

"He's keeping his head really high, but that's just habit. He's nervous about getting caught in the mouth so he takes on that position to protect himself. It will take a while to undo, so don't worry about it right now," Ryan said. "Catch your jump one more time. Nothing but forward and straight."

Tally came back around, correcting the wiggles from Obie to keep him straight to the cross-rail. She held her two-point again just before the jump, grabbed mane, and enjoyed what felt like an oxer effort over the little X.

"Canter, canter, keep him going to the end of the ring, Tal!"

Tally tried her best but Obie broke to the trot a few strides before the end of the ring.

"That's good for today, Tal," Ryan said. "It's so new to him to be using his back. Let's end today—and all your rides—by letting him trot on the buckle so he can stretch out. Just half a lap in each direction for now."

Tally felt a little like a Western rider as she let Obie jog

♘

down the long side on a very loose rein. He stretched his neck out appreciatively, legs sweeping across the ground. Maybe Mac had been right after all. It was fun to see what this little horse could do as he got back into working.

CHAPTER 12

Tally made it to the barn every day for the final week of the summer. Progress with Obie was slow, but steady. Ryan took a client on a horse shopping trip out of town for a few days, so Tally and Maggie exchanged numbers to coordinate hacking times together.

Ryan got back on the Sunday before Labor Day and, for Tally and Maggie's lesson, he had them switch mounts.

Tally couldn't keep from smiling as she trotted around the outdoor ring on Joey. Since he was easily the fanciest pony she'd ever ridden, she felt like she was winning a hack class just trotting around at home. She was hot, as usual, with her vest on, but she tried to put it out of her head. Her parents had issued a warning over dinner the night before. They said that if they ever heard from Ryan or Brenna that she wasn't wearing her vest, they'd ground her for a week. No riding.

"Let them walk a minute, girls," Ryan said, setting jumps on the outside line.

Tally reached down to pat Joey's neck. He let out a big sigh and stretched out at the walk. Across the ring, she watched

Maggie do the same with Obie. He was getting more fit already—no longer flaring his nostrils after their trot work.

"Let's pick up a right lead canter," called Ryan, and Joey perked right up. He was about to do so on his own when Tally shortened her reins and smiled.

"Hang on, buddy, not just yet."

"Good, Tally, make him wait. He clearly knows the word *canter*, but he doesn't decide when it's time to go. You do."

Joey suddenly felt like a race car underneath her, ready to go whenever she gave the signal. The feeling was worlds away from what it was like to ask Obie to step up into a new gait.

Tally pushed Joey to the outside with her inside leg and then just *thought* about cantering—and off he went. Joey's canter had a lot more bounce and animation than she'd expected.

"Let his motion lift your seat out of the saddle a little, Tal. There. Just relax through your thigh and let the movement make your seat light. Think about it like when we jump and that motion closes your hip angle. Maggie, use the whip behind your leg when he sucks back. These guys are like polar opposites, so it's good for you girls to ride both."

As they cantered around, Tally thought about controlling her body and correcting Joey when he got heavy on the forehand. Both Obie and Joey walked a lap before changing direction and picking up the right lead canter.

"Try to sit lighter, Maggie! Driving him forward with your seat is only going to make him hollow and slow down. That's better...use your whip when he sucks back, just a light tap…good. Both of you make a nice, big circle."

Joey wanted to lean on his front end as Tally asked him to make a circle around a single oxer, so she squeezed her fingers and brought her body back. He responded with such smoothness as he lightened his front end, coming up underneath her. So *this* was what it was like to ride a truly made pony, Tally thought.

"Walk a minute, both of you. What's so funny, Mags?" Ryan asked.

"I just can't believe how much leg he takes," Maggie said, breathing hard.

"The goal is to get him to respond to less pressure, not more," Ryan explained. "If you're out of breath at the trot and Obie's not, we need to work on *how* you're asking him to go forward, so that he's more responsive to your leg. Does that make sense?"

Maggie and Tally both nodded.

"Now, I set the outside line as big cross-rails because it helps sharpen their front ends. It also means you *must* ride straight to the middle."

"Those look huge," Maggie said.

"The middle is no taller than a two-foot-six vertical at most," said Ryan. "But the horses will give a bigger effort over it because, visually, it looks taller to them with those high sides. Let's warm up over the cavaletti a couple of times and then we'll try the line. Tally, you go first."

Tally and Maggie both popped over the cavaletti off of

the right lead first, then the left lead.

"That's better, Maggie," said Ryan. "You got the canter you wanted out of your horse, and then you rewarded him by releasing the pressure and not having to work so hard, right? Well done."

Then he nodded to the line of cross-rails.

"You're up, Tal. Straight to the middle."

Tally sat lightly with Joey's big canter, counting down to herself as they reached the first cross-rail. "Three, two, one," she whispered. Joey left the ground in a big effort, as Ryan said he would, rounding through his back. Tally was pretty well-practiced now at controlling her body while jumping. She pressed her hands into Joey's neck and opened her knee angle only, careful not to duck her upper body down. Instead, she concentrated on letting Joey's jump close her hip angle.

"Nice! Now just flow down the line in six."

Land, one, two, three, four, five, six, Tally counted in her mind. It felt like Joey slowed down to study the second X for just a split second and then gave it a beautiful, round effort just like the first.

"Did you feel that? The way he paused just the slightest bit before the out?" Ryan asked.

Tally nodded.

"That's because we school him to jump slowly out over the oxer at the horse shows. It's almost like muscle memory at this point that he gives the out of a line that little pause.

♘

That's exactly what we want. Good for your education, Tally, to know what that feels like. Okay, Maggie, you're up."

Obie and Maggie came around the corner to the first X and Tally could see them both focus in on the middle of the jump.

"Grab mane, keep your leg, and stay straight," said Ryan. Obie jumped up high over the first X, but not as round as Joey.

"Good! Just continue here, he's being protective of his mouth so grab mane again on the out."

Maggie rode up to get the six strides on Obie and he jumped the out of the line just as he'd jumped the in—his head and body high. He landed right, bulging a little toward the gate.

"Good, Maggie, now hold him straight and do a simple change."

Maggie got the change just before the end of the ring and cantered past the gate. Obie looked very proud of himself. Tally was proud of him, too. She wondered how much further they'd be able to take him.

U

· CHAPTER 13 ·

"Welcome back, Johnston West students and staff!" the principal's voice crackled over the loudspeaker as Tally and her friend Kaitlyn Rowe walked up the stairs to their new homeroom. "We hope you had a great summer and we are excited to kick off a new year of learning and discovery."

A chorus of groans rippled through the stairwell.

"*Boooo*," someone shouted and some kids laughed in response.

"Tally!" another voice called from the stairwell. She turned around to see Jacob Viston jogging up the stairs behind her. Jacob and his jumper, Carlo, trained with Ryan as well, trailering in for lessons and shows. Jacob also took lessons on the Oaks school horses.

"Hey!" he said. "I'd much rather be seeing you at the barn than here."

"Jacob, hi," Tally said. Kaitlyn smiled at him.

"We must have different barn schedules. I never see you anymore," Jacob said as they reached the top of the stairs. "Are you guys showing this weekend?"

"I am!" Kaitlyn said.

Tally shrugged. "I'm not sure yet. I might just come watch. How about you?"

"Yup, I'm showing Sweetie, actually," Jacob replied with a smile.

"She's the best," Tally said, returning Jacob's grin. "How is Carlo doing?"

"We sent him to another trainer who specializes in rehabbing horses. He just wasn't staying sound, even at the lower height."

"I'm sorry," Tally said. "That's got to be really hard."

"It's a bummer," Jacob continued. "But he mostly lives in turnout and he's got a new donkey friend in his paddock so he's pretty happy with his life right now. Hopefully the rehab will work and if not, we're talking about donating him somewhere."

"Two minutes until homeroom, people, let's move it!" a teacher bellowed at the end of the hallway.

Jacob rolled his eyes and turned down a hallway lined with yellow lockers. "See you guys later."

At lunchtime, Tally and Kaitlyn found a table in the cafeteria. Sixth graders at their school ate lunch in their homeroom classrooms, and seventh graders had the odd tradition of eating on the floors by the lockers. The cafeteria seating was informally reserved for eighth graders only. No one really knew how the custom got started.

"I thought I'd be happy to finally be eating in the cafeteria," Ava Foster announced as she walked toward Tally and

Kaitlyn's table with her lunch tray. "But I really just think it's stupid. Why are we all following some silly tradition, like sheep? People should eat where they want," she added, popping a tater tot into her mouth as she sat down.

"So why didn't you ever eat where *you* wanted the last two years?" Kaitlyn asked her.

Ava shrugged. "I was a sheep, too."

"You still don't know if you're showing this weekend?" Kaitlyn asked Tally, eager to change the subject from sheep back to horses.

"Nope," Tally said, piercing the top of her juice box with a straw. "Ryan's been in and out of the barn on horse shopping trips so we haven't talked about it. Maybe I'd show Obie though."

"Who's Obie?" Ava asked. Ava used to own a pony named Danny (who had one of Tally's favorite show names—Stonelea Dance Party), and they showed in the medium pony hunter division before Ava took up gymnastics in place of riding.

"He's a new project horse at the barn," Tally began. "He needs a new job. I don't think he's ever been to a horse show before."

"You're a better rider than I was, always sitting on something new," Ava said.

"Oh please," said Tally with a little laugh. "You know what happened the one time I tried to show Danny!" About a year ago, Tally got to catch-ride Ava's old pony while Ryan worked on selling him. At Tally's very first A-show, Danny stopped at the first jump—pilot error—and she fell off. That was the beginning and the end of her show day, right there.

"Danny wasn't easy. I hope he's being good to his new kid," Ava said. "You know, the balance beam doesn't have an opinion of its own."

"Well, that's boring," said Kaitlyn and all three of them laughed.

The girls were trading stories about riding and gymnastics when someone else appeared at their table.

"Is this seat taken?" Jacob asked with a smile.

"No, sit down!" said Tally.

"But…aren't you in *seventh* grade?" asked Ava.

Jacob nodded.

"What happened to your sheep theory?" Kaitlyn asked Ava. Jacob looked confused.

"We were talking about how everyone just accepts the unspoken rule about seventh graders sitting on the floor," Tally said as Jacob pulled a brown paper bag out of his backpack.

"Oh, that's so last year," Jacob said with a little wave of his hand. "I know lots of seventh graders who are sitting with their eighth-grade friends. It's about time we broke with tradition, don't you think?"

No one disagreed with him.

CHAPTER 14

"*Happy birthday*, Tally!"

Mac, Maggie, and Jacob all jumped up from behind the trunks in the Field Ridge tack room, startling Tally so much she dropped the bag of carrots and the saddle pads she was holding. Mac giggled and came over to hug her.

"That was just mean," said Mac, "scaring her on her birthday like that!"

"We didn't mean to scare you, Tal, we just wanted it to be a surprise," Maggie said, presenting Tally with a box of cupcakes. Someone had written "13" in sparkly blue ink across the box.

"That's okay," Tally said, her cheeks red but her heart full from her friends' sweet gesture.

"Open your presents!" Jacob said, handing her a pile of gifts next.

Tally smiled and tore the shiny gold paper off of the awkwardly wrapped presents, one by one. Gift wrapping did not appear to come naturally to her friends. It was pretty cute.

Inside the wrapping were three grooming brushes—a brand Tally had deemed too expensive to buy for herself.

She'd mentioned the brushes to Mac forever ago, having read a great write-up about them in *The Plaid Horse.*

"Because you love grooming so much!" Mac said triumphantly as Tally ran the soft bristles across her palm. "Do you like them?"

"I *love* them!" Tally said, feeling a little choked up as she hugged each of her friends. "You guys are so sweet, thank you."

"You're welcome," Maggie and Jacob said in unison.

Jacob looked at the bakery box. "Is ten in the morning too early to eat cupcakes?"

Later on, when it was time for lessons, Tally was happy to get into the ring with Jacob again. It had been a while since they'd ridden together. Now that everyone was riding after school, slightly bigger group lessons would be the norm.

This particular lesson for Tally, Jacob, and Maggie was mostly flatwork, but with the schooling show coming up in just a few days, Ryan set up some jumps specifically for Jacob to practice—he was going to show Sweetie in an equitation division and the medal.

"Pick up your right lead canter and jump your gate here," Ryan said, pointing to the white gate set on the diagonal. "Ask Sweetie for the left lead in the air, and if she doesn't give it to you, sit up and step out for the change. Shape your left-hand turn and jump the oxer out of the outside line. Canter past the ingate and then get your trot, turn up the middle, and catch this trot jump here."

Jacob nodded and invisibly cued Sweetie into her right

lead canter. In typical Sweetie fashion, she briefly flattened her ears and swished her tail but then settled into a nice canter and a more content expression.

"Direct left rein in the air and look left, Jacob. Be sure you give a nice release with your right hand."

When Tally rode Sweetie, she felt like the little horse preferred to rush off the ground, but Jacob had her going with such impulsion from behind that Sweetie actually jumped the gate slowly and carefully off the ground. Jacob set his right hand in a crest release on Sweetie's neck and looked left while directing his left rein toward his hip. Sweetie landed with another swish of her tail, but she was on her left lead.

"That's the ride! Step out a bit in your turn...there. Now just let the oxer come to you."

Tally envied Jacob's deep heels and beautiful, upright posture as he and Sweetie approached the oxer. She could tell that Sweetie wanted to pull Jacob toward it but he balanced her so well. They cleared the oxer and cantered through the turn near the gate toward their trot jump.

"Don't muscle her down into the trot, think of squeezing your hand and sinking into the tack...good. Do the trot jump just like that at the show. Okay, Maggie, you're up!"

After the lesson, Tally, Maggie, and Mac gathered on the Field Ridge aisle, chatting about that trot jump.

"Obie is always happy to trot at a moment's notice, but I think it would have been hard to get the trot in time on any other horse," Tally said.

☩

"Or pony," Maggie said with a laugh. "I couldn't even get Joey down to a trot the first time! He cantered right over it."

Mac, who'd stayed to watch the lesson, gave her pony a scratch on his withers. "Joey thinks trot jumps are silly. Don't you, boy?"

"Why trot any jump when you could be cantering?" joked Maggie.

Once everyone had cooled out their mounts, Tally led Obie out to the paddocks for night turnout. Mac came with her.

"I've been meaning to tell you, I got to ride Joey in my lesson the other day. It was so much fun." Tally said. "Ryan had me and Maggie trade horses, so she rode Obie."

"Oh, yay!" Mac replied. "He was a good boy for you?"

"*So* good. I knew he was amazing, but getting to ride him was just the best," Tally continued. "We jumped cross-rails set on, like, the top hole of the standards. Ryan said it helps sharpen their front end and make them jump nice and round. Anyway, it was like he measured the strides down the outside line *for* me, he's such a good boy."

"Um, yeah," Mac said, an odd expression settling into her face.

"I mean, I only had to *think* about slowing down when I jumped into a line and he did it for me. Your pony is just awesome."

"Yup." Mac was definitely acting weird now. But Tally couldn't figure out why. It was quiet between them as Tally opened the gate for Obie, took off his halter, and closed the gate behind her as she slipped out and clipped the chain shut.

"So..." Tally began, feeling at a loss for words around her best barn friend for maybe the first time ever. "Are you excited to ride? Only a week away, right?"

Mac nodded, taking her phone out of the back pocket of her jean shorts. "My mom is going to be here soon so I better go. See you later, Tal. Hope you had a good birthday," she added, hastily turning to head back for the barn. Tally stood at the gate, Obie's halter still in her hand, wondering what had just happened.

CHAPTER 15

Between each class at school on Friday, Tally checked her phone to see if Mac had responded to her texts from the night before. But there was nothing.

"I just don't know what I could have said that upset her," she told her friends in the cafeteria after relaying the story about what happened with Mac.

"I actually think it's kind of obvious," said Ava. Tally, Kaitlyn, and Jacob all looked at her.

"Well, tell me!" said Tally. "What is it?"

"You basically told her how easy her pony is to ride, and how he did the work for you, measuring the lines," Ava said.

"But I didn't mean it like *that*," Tally insisted.

"I know you didn't," Ava continued. "But Mac tried a bunch of ponies that didn't work out before they found Joey. She's probably self-conscious that you think he's a push-button ride. Or that she's not a good rider."

Tally felt like Ava punched her in the stomach. She'd gushed about Joey to Mac because she'd never ridden a pony so fancy and well-schooled before. She never even thought about Mac's riding as it related to the way Joey performed.

She just thought the pony was amazing.

That night, Tally texted and called Mac again but got no response. She felt awful for hurting her friend's feelings. Watching a movie with her parents, Tally tapped her phone so obsessively to see if there was a reply that her mom took the phone away. Stacy turned it off and stuck it in a kitchen drawer for the night.

The next afternoon, as Tally flatted Obie around the outdoor ring, she felt super distracted. She hadn't heard anything from Mac in nearly two days—easily the longest they'd gone without talking. Tally went through the motions in the outdoor ring while Ryan taught Kaitlyn and another couple of riders. Everyone wrapped up around the same time, dismounting in the center of the ring. As the others walked out, Ryan called Tally over.

"What's on your mind, kiddo? You don't seem like yourself today."

Tally opened her mouth to tell Ryan that everything was fine, but a sob escaped instead. Embarrassed, she turned away from her trainer as the tears spilled down her cheeks.

"Hey," he said, his voice soft and kind. "What's going on?"

Tally told him everything—what she'd said to Mac on her birthday, as well as Mac's reaction and her silence in response to Tally's texts and calls. Ryan sat down on one end of the top rail of a vertical and Tally sat on the other end, holding the buckle of her reins in one hand. Obie lazily swished his tail.

⚘

"Riders tend to gravitate toward feeling or thinking, Tal," Ryan explained. "The best catch riders feel and *then* think. It's natural for you to feel the horses and you understand them that way. It gives you a real leg up in this sport, having such a natural feel. Not everyone has that."

"What type of rider is Mac?" Tally asked between sniffles.

"Mac is more of a thinker. Plenty of riders are. She thinks so much about her riding and she tries so hard that it can interfere with the feel sometimes. Joey seemed really easy to you to ride, right?"

Tally nodded.

"He wasn't so easy for her when we got him. Now, they've come a long way, and Mac has really put in the work. I'm proud of her. I think what happened here is the way you described Joey made Mac feel badly about herself as a rider."

Tally felt like her stomach was twisting into knots. She never meant to hurt her friend's feelings.

"I know you'd never hurt her feelings on purpose," Ryan said. "She's sensitive about this kind of thing. Some riders have to work harder than others just to end up in the same place. Does that make sense?"

Tally nodded again.

"She'll come around, Tal. I know you guys are great friends."

Before Tally's dad came to the barn to pick her up late that afternoon, she slipped into the tack shop. If Mac wouldn't respond to texts, Tally thought, she'd have to try something else. Tally fished a twenty-dollar bill out of her backpack (she always saved her birthday and holiday money to spend on horse stuff) and bought a braided leather bracelet with a silver horseshoe. She'd seen Mac checking it out the last time they were in the tack shop together. Then she ripped out a sheet of notebook paper, and wrote a quick note to her friend:

Mac,

I am so sorry if what I said about Joey upset you. I didn't mean to do that, but I feel awful that I did. I think you are an incredible rider and it is my dream to show at the big shows like you one day and to have the presence you have in the ring. You actually make it look easy. Please don't be mad at me. I can't wait for you to get to ride again soon.

xoxo,
Tally

Tally and her dad stopped at Mac's house before going home. There was no car in the driveway, thankfully, so Tally wrapped up the bracelet inside the note and dropped it through the mail slot in Mac's front door without needing to have any awkward conversations.

There was nothing left to do but wait.

· CHAPTER 16 ·

"Junior equitation riders, please make your way to the ring. We're going to start with the flat class today. Junior equitation riders, five minutes until you flat."

Tally sat in the bleachers to watch Jacob and Kaitlyn at the Oaks schooling show. Ryan had given her the option to show Obie, but an away show was coming up the following week, and her parents said she had to choose between the two. Tally and Ryan were both curious about how Obie would react to a show environment away from home, so they opted to wait for the next one. Tally could sit and watch a horse show all day long. She was almost as happy to be cheering on her friends as she would be showing herself.

Jacob entered the ring on Sweetie with Kaitlyn behind him riding Scout, the big bay gelding from the lesson program. The judge asked the class to trot (both posting and sitting), canter tracking left, and then halt. Kaitlyn got a clean, quick halt out of Scout. Jacob did a great job of hiding how hard it was to halt Sweetie out of the canter. The mare opened her mouth and shook her head into the halt, but Tally knew that didn't always mean her rider was being harsh with their hands. Sweetie was a horse who would never be thrilled about downward transitions. And she was definitely not a fan of halting in a busy show ring.

"Riders, walk, all walk and change direction," said the announcer. "Drop your irons and trot, please."

A hush fell over the spectators. A couple of riders in the ring swiveled their heads to look at the others, confirming what they'd heard. The judge hadn't specified sitting or posting trot, so the riders made their own choices. Both Kaitlyn and Jacob were sitting, as were two other riders. Another two were posting.

"Sit and walk, riders, please sit and walk…Now canter, riders, all canter."

Tally pinned the class in her mind. She was sure the judge noticed when Sweetie didn't want to halt. How much that hurt Jacob's score would depend on what the other riders did. Tally mentally put Jacob in first or second. Kaitlyn was late getting her right lead canter so Tally had her in fourth.

"Riders, we have your results for class fourteen, junior equitation on the flat. In first place, number 54, Jacob Viston, riding Sweet Talker."

Tally clapped and let out a little whoop for Jacob, who grinned as a young rider in braids and bows reached up to hand him a blue ribbon. Kaitlyn ended up third. The equitation over fences class began right after they finished pinning the flat.

"First in the ring for junior equitation over fences is

number 22, Mallory Cummings, riding Cosmo."

Tally didn't know Mallory beyond watching her ride in the flat class. She'd come in fourth. And now she was putting in a strong round over fences. Mallory had a great position and she was finding all of her jumps and getting clean transitions out of Cosmo for their trot jump and their halt at the end of the course.

Kaitlyn was next, and she had a solid course, too. Jacob went after her, and was able to replicate what Tally had seen in their last lesson together. Through the rollback on course, similar to the one they'd practiced with Ryan, Jacob turned his head to look for the second jump before they'd even completed the first. That was always difficult for Tally, who had a hard time turning her head early enough when she had to look for a tight turn.

The course was a great one for Jacob and Sweetie until the very end. Where Cosmo and Scout had halted several strides away from the last jump, Jacob couldn't get Sweetie back until they'd nearly hit the end of the ring. He did get her to halt straight though, and he held the halt for a couple of seconds before walking out of the ring. Tally applauded and wondered what the judge would do with that.

Three more riders tackled the course next, all with bright spots and small mistakes of their own. Tally wasn't going to play judge on this one. It was too hard to figure out how the errors measured up.

"First place and congratulations goes to number 22, Mallory

Cummings, aboard Cosmo," said the announcer. "Second place is 54, Jacob Viston and Sweet Talker."

"Whoo!" Tally hollered, clapping for Jacob and Kaitlyn, who was called next for another third-place ribbon.

There was a pony equitation division before the medal, so Tally hopped up from the bleachers to meet Jacob and Kaitlyn outside the ring for pictures. Brenna had set up a photo op area by the outdoor ring and Tally wanted to make use of it for her friends. On her way out, she spotted Mallory and Cosmo.

"Congrats," Tally said to Mallory.

"Thanks," Mallory said, grinning and hugging Cosmo. It struck Tally how much easier it was to just be friends with everyone at the barn. It was so much more complicated in school. She felt a pang about Mac and hoped that Ryan was right—that it was only a matter of time before they moved past their misunderstanding. Tally really missed her friend.

· CHAPTER 17 ·

At the end of the show day, Kaitlyn had her two thirds from the equitation division and another third-place ribbon from a big, competitive medal class. Jacob was champion in the equitation division and was fourth in the medal—he had a couple of deep distances and a late change. Both were thrilled with how the day had gone.

Ryan had more clients showing so Tally wouldn't be taking a lesson that afternoon, but she planned to flat Obie in the small indoor, the ring left open on home show days so boarders could ride.

Tally trotted Obie in both directions, making circles around the jumps set up in the ring. Then she trotted on a serpentine, changing the bend frequently through the turns and keeping the little horse in front of her leg.

"Good boy," she told Obie with a pat, taking a walk break.

"He looks great, Tally. Remember when you could hardly get him to canter when he first came?" Isabelle rode up next to them on her junior hunter, Pip.

Tally laughed. "Yes, he's really teaching me to use my leg the right way."

"Are you showing with us next week?" Isabelle asked.

Tally nodded. "Yes, but we're still doing simple changes on him, so I'm not sure what sort of division we'll do."

"Baby greens, maybe, if they have it at this show?" Isabelle suggested.

"Maybe," Tally said, patting Obie's neck again. "Whatever we do, I'm just excited to take him off the property and see what he thinks of horse shows."

After Isabelle struck out on her own along the rail, Tally asked Obie to canter. The dressage whip felt less foreign in her hand now, and it was a useful tool to have when the horse wasn't responsive to her leg. In their last lesson, Ryan had them canter three laps in both directions to continue improving Obie's fitness. That had been in the large outdoor ring, so Tally figured they could do the same in the small indoor.

Obie was surprisingly willing to canter laps to the left. He seemed a little lazier to the right, so Tally added a circle and cantered a rail on the ground to try to keep his interest. She didn't even need to use the dressage whip.

Once the last lap was complete, Tally asked Obie to go right into his trot on the buckle to stretch out. A real creature of habit, Obie had come to expect this little jog at the end of their rides. He let out a big exhale and stretched his neck out low as Tally let the reins all the way out. They made a big, looping figure eight around the ring and then walked a couple of laps.

⚘

Back on the aisle, the cross ties were occupied so Tally untacked Obie in his stall—saddle first so she could hold the reins, as was her newly-ingrained habit. He dropped his head and turned toward her, a classic Obie signal that he wanted affection.

Tally giggled as she leaned her saddle up against the stall wall to indulge Obie in some rubs and snuggles.

"Does that feel good, buddy?" she asked. Obie closed his eyes and stuck his head out while Tally scratched around his ears. She loved learning each horse's favorite scratching spots.

"Hey," said a voice in the doorway.

It was Mac.

"Hi," said Tally, her heart instantly racing at the sight of her friend.

"No more sling," Mac said, waving her arm away from her body. "And I get my cast cut off on Thursday morning. Then I'm riding after school."

"That's so exciting," said Tally, closing Obie's door and hanging up his halter. He popped his head over the stall door, as if he were anticipating this conversation as much as Tally.

"Thanks for the bracelet. That was really sweet of you," Mac added. Tally glanced at Mac's wrists. She wasn't wearing it.

"Of course," Tally began, eager to clear the air even further with her friend. But Mac spoke first.

"I'm going to groom Joey one-handed," she said, waving her cast again. "See ya."

♘

Tally felt like the wind had been knocked out of her. "Bye."

That was it? It felt like she and Mac were merely acquaintances now, rather than the great friends they'd been for the past year.

The next day at school, Tally tried to push the interaction with Mac from her mind. If Mac wasn't ready to move on yet, what could Tally do?

Kaitlyn chatted excitedly all through lunch about the horse show.

"Scout was such a good boy and there were great parts of both our trips, but I know I can do better," she said. "I can't wait for the next show in the series. I'm going for one of those big year-end ribbons this year!"

"I know what you mean," Jacob added. "I let Sweetie rush past a couple distances because part of my brain turns off when I'm showing. If I ride her in a show the way I ride her in lessons we could do even better."

"I'm not riding Obie all that well in lessons yet, so I'm not even sure why we're showing," Tally added with a laugh.

"Sounds like you've made so much progress though," said Jacob. "You said you couldn't get him to canter when you started riding him!"

Tally laughed. "People keep saying that! It's true, though. I was getting five strides of canter out of him, max."

"And now you're jumping courses," said Jacob.

"Not always from the canter," added Tally with a grin.

"Eh, it's great for their stifles to do trot jumps," said Jacob.

"How do you guys know all this stuff?" Kaitlyn asked them.

"Horse nerds," Tally said with a shug. "I don't know, I just can't get enough of it. I'm reading horse books constantly. Luckily my parents don't seem to notice that they aren't textbooks!"

CHAPTER 18

On Tally's first shift of the week, she and another junior working student, Kelsey, were tasked with grooming the smaller school ponies.

"These guys have been getting a quick once-over by the staff, or a very gentle grooming by their tiny riders," Brenna explained. "But they could use a lot more currying. I made up a list next to the bathing list by the stairs. Those ponies need a thorough grooming at least twice a week. You can each pick a couple to do and check them off the list for today."

Tally and Kelsey glanced at each other and then took off jogging down the aisle. There were certain school ponies that everyone just got a little more excited about.

Kelsey reached the board first, grabbed a pen, and drew a line through Little Bit's name.

"Got her!" she said, elbowing Tally lightly.

"I wasn't even going for Lil. She tries to bite me," Tally replied, playfully grabbing the pen out of Kelsey's hand. "I wanted Lati anyway."

"Good, we understand each other then," Kelsey said, grinning. "See ya, Tal."

Tally went into the school tack room for Lati's grooming box. The boxes lined the long wall underneath the saddle racks, each one labeled with the horse or pony's name.

It would have been a lot easier to just use shared grooming supplies for a big lesson program, Brenna had once explained to her. But equine skin conditions like scratches and fungus were contagious and could easily spread with shared tools. Plus, grooming supplies weren't always one-size-fits-all. A thin-skinned Thoroughbred doesn't need a metal currycomb like a fuzzy pony might, for example. So the barn management decided long ago that each horse would get their own supplies. Boots, wraps, or earplugs specific to each horse were stored in their individual grooming boxes, too.

Lati (short for Gelati) lived in one of the stalls on the outside of the aisle—the most coveted stalls, Tally always thought, since the horses could stick their heads out of the large picture windows facing the hill and the big indoor and outdoor rings. Lesson kids would sometimes walk along the grass outside the barn windows, stopping at each stall to sit in the windowsill and pat the horses or feed them carrots.

"Hi, sweet girl," Tally said as she reached Lati's stall. Lati was a sturdy, stocky little leopard Appaloosa pony, with brown and black spots all over her white coat. Tally thought she was super cute, but there was something about Lati's appearance that really captured the little kids at the barn. On more than one occasion, Tally overheard a small child gasp in Lati's presence, calling her the most beautiful horse in the world. It must be the spots, Tally thought with a grin.

Lati was gazing out her big picture window when Tally arrived. "Come see what I have for you, pony," Tally said. Lati turned to look at her and paused, as if considering whether it was worth abandoning her view. Evidently, it was, and the pony ambled over to where Tally stood in the doorway.

Tally produced a horse muffin from her pocket and Lati eagerly gobbled it up. Tally threaded her fingers through Lati's thick forelock and rubbed her forehead. Lati stood totally still, enjoying the undivided attention.

First, Tally picked out the pony's bare feet. Then she slid the pink grooming mitt onto her hand, but immediately tossed it aside when she felt something crawling inside. The mitt landed in the stall shavings with a little *thwack* and a stunned spider scurried out of it. Tally and Lati exchanged a glance and Tally shrugged.

"Let's try that again, huh?"

Tally shook the grooming mitt in case anything else was hanging out inside, and put it back on her right hand. She rubbed it all over the mare's coat in circular motions. Lati stood still as a statue—clearly practiced at making even the smallest riders feel comfortable around her.

"Do you like that, sweet girl?"

Tally used the soft mitt on Lati's face, and a little plume of dust and fine hair escaped. Lati closed her eyes and sighed. Tally was so happy to help the pony feel good. And she loved how much Brenna cared about the school horses' well-being.

After Tally followed up with the stiff brush and then a soft brush, she dug through all the pockets in her denim shorts. Lati's ears perked up as Tally found a mint in a crinkly wrapper. Lati took a step closer, her eyes trained on Tally.

"Sorry, girl, it's all sticky, hang on!" Tally said with a giggle, impressed at the school pony's polite demeanor.

Tally felt like she could have spent her entire shift in Lati's stall, just enjoying her company, but there was more work to be done. She groomed a bay pony named Toots next, who danced around a whole lot more than Lati had, despite being tied in the stall with Tally's trusty quick-release knot.

Tally bathed two horses on the list after that, and just as her shift was wrapping up, she ran into Ryan on the aisle.

"Hey, we haven't discussed the show yet, have we?" he asked.

"Not yet," Tally said, eager to hear what her trainer had in mind.

"We're going to Bird Creek next weekend. It's a big show barn about fifty miles north of here, so we won't ship in the way we do with some of the other shows," Ryan explained. "It's a two-day show, but the divisions run in full on either Saturday or Sunday. You'll show Obie on Sunday only, so the horses will have stalls there Saturday night. Lupe and I will stay overnight at the hotel and do night check and all that good stuff. You guys can stay Saturday night too, or just drive up early Sunday. You won't show until Sunday afternoon."

"Got it," said Tally, smiling. She couldn't wait to get back in the show ring.

U

"Maggie shows Sunday too, so you guys can coordinate the trip if you want. I'm going to enter you and Obie in the limit hunters. It's a two-foot division and they don't penalize for simple changes. We'll work this week on asking for the lead in the air and getting a quick, clean simple when you need it. Don't feel like the two-foot is a step down. Any more than that, and you're going to be up against horses with a change. This is a good height for a horse that's never been to a show before, and it still gives you a chance to be competitive before we put the changes on him."

"Sounds great," Tally said. "I'm so excited."

"Good," Ryan replied. "Make sure you get on the schedule for a few lessons this week."

· CHAPTER 19 ·

Tally checked the white board in the Field Ridge tack room right when she got to the barn the next day. It was just her and Mac in the 4:00 p.m. lesson. She put Obie on the cross ties to groom him but kept craning her neck to see if Mac had arrived. By 3:55, there was still no sign of Mac, so Tally figured she'd gotten up to the ring early to walk around.

Up at the outdoor ring, Mac was, in fact, already walking around on Joey and chatting with Ryan. Tally could see she was fanning herself with her hand—her first ride in a body protector was probably just as hot as Tally's. It might have been mid-September, but it still felt very much like summer. Maggie sat on the bleachers to watch the lesson.

Tally mounted up, making sure that Obie didn't walk off until she was ready. The habit had become nearly second nature now.

"Hey, Tally, walk on over here," said Ryan. She wished she could catch Mac's eye or just share a moment with her friend.

"It's time," Ryan said with a wink, holding up a pair of spurs. "I can't really believe we haven't done this yet, but I'm starting you off with a rounded pair. Your leg and foot position is solid, but just remember that when you turn your toes out, you're using the spur in his side. Only do that when you need it. Your spur backs up your leg the way the dressage whip does. I don't want you going to the spur first."

Tally took her feet out of the stirrups and Ryan slid the spurs around the backs of her heels, securing the spur straps under the arches of her feet. Then he bucked them on the tops of her boots and gave Obie a pat on the shoulder.

"Let's start with some leg yields at the walk," Ryan said. "Tally, if Obie resists or won't move forward off your leg, turn your toe out and see what kind of reaction you get from the spur."

Obie stuck his head in the air when Tally asked him to yield left, off the rail, so Tally turned her right toe out as Ryan had explained. Obie lowered his head in response, his hind end came up underneath him, and he moved smoothly to the left.

"That's it! Now turn your toe right back in since he listened," Ryan said. "Remember, you don't ever want to use your spur unnecessarily. Both of you girls can leg yield back to the rail now."

They practiced leg yielding and bending in both directions. Tally knew they were warming up slowly both for her sake with the new spurs and for Mac's sake. A month was a long time to be out of the saddle.

"Mac, start us off on a serpentine at the trot. Both of you really think about staying straight across the ring. Pick a point and ride straight to it, don't let them drift."

Tally followed Mac on the serpentine, catching glimpses of her friend here and there. Mac was riding with a brace of some sort on her wrist.

After a walk break, they cantered for a bit, incorporating a rail on the quarter line to canter over.

"How are ya feeling, Mac Attack?" asked Ryan.

"So hot," said Mac, nearly breathless. "And so tired. This feels like major cardio to me today."

"It'll come back fast, I promise," Ryan told her.

Mac and Tally started their jump school over a rail, set on a line with a raised cavaletti after it.

"I haven't walked this yet. How many strides does it look like to you?" Ryan asked. Tally and Mac looked at each other and exchanged shy smiles.

"Anyone?"

"Um...six?" Tally asked.

"Okay. Go ride it and make it happen in six."

Tally cued Obie into his left lead canter, legging him up to get to a good rhythm.

They met the rail just right and Tally counted in her mind: *land, one, two, three—oh there's no way this is six strides—four, five, jump.*

"Huh. Seems more like a five than a six, huh?" Ryan asked with a wide grin. "Give it a shot, Mac."

Mac and Joey cantered along the long side of the ring and turned left up the middle toward the exercise. "Whoa," Mac said when Joey jumped over the rail strong. Tally watched her sink into the tack and close her fingers. Joey condensed his stride and met the cavaletti just right. He seemed happy to have his person back, Tally thought, smiling to herself.

They did the exercise a couple more times, alternating between five and six strides to work on adjustability.

"Keep that bouncy, up-and-down canter before you get to the rail," Ryan called as Tally cantered in on Obie. He cleared the rail and immediately broke to the trot. It took another two tries for Tally to condense his stride while keeping the canter.

"Not as easy as it looks, right?" Ryan asked. "Now let's jump the outside line in six and you'll see how easily it comes up." He took the back rail down from the oxer so both jumps were on the smaller side. Then he took a towel from a chair in the ring and draped it over the rail on the first jump of the line. He dragged two flower boxes from the wall and put them under the rail of the second jump.

"Obie is really used to the plain jumps in this ring," said Ryan. "I want to give him something to stare at so it's less of a shock at the horse show. Mac, get this line first. If you do it in six, let Joey walk out and we'll quit with that for today."

Mac legged Joey into the canter and they approached the line. Tally thought that Mac might look a tiny bit looser over-all than usual, but it was hardly a noticeable change. After an injury and a month off of riding, she barely missed a beat.

"Only think about his canter rhythm, Mac," Ryan said. "Count it out in your head: one, two, one, two. Keep the rhythm consistent and both jumps will come right up for you."

Joey jumped into the line and landed nice and forward. Mac eased back into the saddle.

"Put your shoulders back!" called Ryan.

Mac and Joey got a little deep to the out, but nothing major. Joey swapped his lead smoothly before the corner and Mac rubbed his neck for a stride or two before bringing him back down to the walk.

"Nice, Mac! Like nothing ever happened," Ryan said.

Mac rolled her eyes but she was smiling. "It was just one line."

"Sure, but you put in a whole flat lesson and then jumped around a little after four weeks of no riding. I'm proud of you, kiddo."

Mac let her reins out to the buckle and bent down to hug Joey's neck.

"You're up, Tal."

Tally asked Obie to canter, and as soon as they were straight to the vertical, she felt him stare at the towel on the jump rail. He sucked back, his canter rhythm all but disappearing.

"Leg him forward!" Ryan shouted.

Obie broke to the trot and Tally turned her toes out to use her spurs.

"Just trot it, you're fine," said Ryan. Still staring at the towel, Obie launched high up over the vertical, rounding his back. He landed in a heap, barely cantering.

"Leg, leg, leg!" said Ryan.

Tally got a few canter strides out of Obie but lost count of how many. They jumped out awkwardly over the second jump of the line.

"Come right around and do it again, Tal. Have more pace through the turn and the minute you feel him suck back, tap him behind your leg with the crop."

Tally did just that, and Obie responded by tossing his head a little, but he listened to her and cantered all the way up to the vertical this time.

"Good, keep going!" called Ryan.

Tally managed to canter the whole line this time, adding a stride and jumping out in six. She asked Obie for a simple change after the out and cantered away with some pace before bringing him down to a walk.

"So, he stared a little more than we were expecting, huh?" Ryan said. Tally nodded. "We'll have another couple of lessons, and you'll trot in to the lines at the horse show. That's why we're putting him in the division we did. We'll just keep building on this. Good job today, girls, I'll see you tomorrow."

CHAPTER 20

"Do you think those jumps are going to eat you, or what?" Tally asked Obie, who looked at her curiously on the cross ties with that sweet, soft expression. As part of her standard warm weather grooming, Tally towel-dried his sweaty girth area. Mac had to leave right after the lesson, so Maggie was on cool out duty with Joey on the cross ties in front of Obie.

"He's so cute though," Maggie said. "Do you think it's just the first time he's seen anything but plain jumps?"

"Probably," Tally said with a laugh. "I just hope I can get him over them in the show ring."

"You got him over everything today," Maggie noted. She was right. Ryan pointed out that Obie did suck back and stare when jumps looked new or different to him, but if she asked him to go forward, he always did. Rider confidence made a big difference on this horse.

Tally and Maggie chatted about Mac's first ride back and Tally felt awash with sadness. Mac was being perfectly cordial and friendly with her, but things weren't the same. Far from it.

"I'm so glad we're going together on Sunday," Maggie said, changing the subject to the upcoming Bird Creek show. "I've never done a rated show before. Actually, I've never done any shows other than the ones we have here."

Tally smiled. "I was in the exact same boat a year ago. I was so worried about it, but it's really not that different from the shows we do here."

"Really?" asked Maggie.

"Yup. I thought it would be a whole different world. But horse shows are horse shows. The rated ones have more decorated jumps and most of the horses and ponies have a big stride and a good lead change and they're fancy and all that, but it's not as different as I thought it would be."

"That's a relief," Maggie said, unclipping Joey and leading him to his stall. "So, I don't need to wear anything new or pack anything different?"

"Nope. Ryan is a stickler for having your hairnet pushed up to your hairline. And your boot socks can't stick out over your boots, but he's just as strict about those things at the schooling shows," Tally said, blushing at the memory of her brightly-colored lucky socks poking out of her boots at her first A-rated show.

Maggie nodded. "Do you think the horses will get braided?"

"Yes, and that part's awesome," Tally said, fully grinning now. "It just makes you feel...dressed up. I love seeing them braided."

"I can't wait," Maggie said.

That Sunday morning, before the sun came up, Tally's mom drove to Maggie's house to pick her up for the show at

Bird Creek. Maggie's mom stood in the front doorway and waved as Maggie jogged down her driveway.

Opening the passenger door, Maggie tossed her backpack inside and plopped down after it. "Thanks for the ride, Mrs. Hart," she said cheerfully.

"My pleasure," said Tally's mom. "It's great to meet you. I've heard so much about you from Tally."

The girls chatted in the back seat for the entire hour and fifteen-minute car ride until the showgrounds came into view. Bird Creek was a much larger facility than the other places Tally had shown, complete with the big horse show tents, half a dozen rings, and sprawling grounds.

"How are we ever going to find Ryan?" Maggie asked.

"I was wondering the same thing," said Tally. Her mom waved her phone from the front seat.

"Ryan told me exactly where to park," she said. "I'll be dropping you off right at the temporary stalls where the horses are stabled." After a slow drive through the showgrounds, stopping for passing horses and golf carts, they arrived at the Field Ridge setup. A Field Ridge banner in the barn colors, hunter green and cream, hung above a little seating area decorated with pots of mums. The banner was lined with ribbons won by Field Ridge riders the day before—so many that they partially covered Ryan's name, stitched onto the right side of the banner.

"No pressure," Maggie said dryly, nodding at the ribbons.

"Good morning!" Ryan said as he turned the corner at the

end of the stalls. "How are you, Mrs. Hart?" Obie poked his head out. He looked positively adorable in his braids.

"I'm well, thank you, how are you, Ryan? And could you point me in the direction of some coffee?"

While Ryan directed Tally's mom to a nearby food stand, Tally showed Maggie where to put her things in the tack stall.

"I'm sorry, Tal, but this is nothing like a schooling show."

"It's exciting, right?" said Tally. "But I promise once you get on and start warming up, it doesn't feel all that different. Want to take a walk around?"

Maggie did, and hearing her observations of the horse show reminded Tally of how far she'd come in such a short time riding with Ryan. Even if she was still pretty starstruck by her surroundings at a big show.

"Um, every single horse here is prettier than the last," Maggie whispered as the girls walked up the path that ran alongside each of the rings. Grooms and riders led a parade of horses and ponies to and from the rings for the first classes of the morning.

"I know," Tally replied dreamily.

"They are *so* shiny," Maggie said. "I love all the braided reins and the perfect, fluffy white saddle pads. Is it a requirement to braid the horses?"

"At the A-rated shows it is. Well, maybe more like an unspoken requirement," Tally told her. "I don't think it's in the rule book, but everyone braids at a big show. At one-day shows and B shows, some people don't braid. You won't see any unbraided here."

The girls had reached the ring at the end of the show-grounds, labeled "Grand Prix Ring" on the outside of the judge's box. They watched a few rounds of the children's jumpers, giggling about how long the course was and how easy it would be to get lost on the way to the combination.

By late morning, Tally and Maggie were both warming up in the schooling area. They'd been lucky enough to get in when it wasn't very busy, so Obie could take in his first horse show without strange horses whizzing past him from all directions.

"How's Joey?" Tally asked.

"He's...exactly the same as he is at home," Maggie said with a little laugh. She seemed more relaxed now than when they first arrived. "So, it's just me who's nervous I guess. How's Obie?"

"Not as looky as I thought he'd be," Tally said. "I guess we'll see what happens in the show ring, but so far, so good."

Ryan had both girls jump a vertical and an oxer a few times before having Tally dismount and give Obie a rest. Obie had two divisions to wait so Lupe, the Field Ridge groom, took him back to the stalls for some water.

Tally walked alongside Ryan to the Dover ring, one of the smaller rings of the six on the property. Maggie was showing Joey in the children's pony division to close out her short-term lease.

The children's pony division and Tally's limit hunter

division both jumped the same courses, so Ryan talked the girls through them together.

"Tally, there's another division in between Maggie's and yours," Ryan said. "I put you in that hack so you can give Obie a tour of the ring before you jump around." Tally was relieved to have a chance to show Obie the horse-eating flower boxes and brush before they'd have to jump them.

"These jumps are gorgeous," Maggie whispered. "I love the flower baskets hanging from the standards. I know Joey isn't going to care about any of the decorations, but I'm impressed!"

A few trips before Maggie, a girl of about ten walked into the ring and picked up her canter on a dapple-gray pony with an expression Tally would recognize anywhere.

Goose.

"In for a first hunter trip, this is Goose, ridden by Olivia Motes," said the announcer.

Tally watched as the little rider piloted Goose around the course, the pony looking even more smooth and relaxed than he'd been just a few months prior. As they did their closing circle, Tally suddenly felt the urge to run from the ring. If Goose recognized her when he and Olivia left the ring, she felt like her heart would break. And if the pony didn't remember who she was...Tally couldn't decide what was worse.

"Be right back," she squeaked to Ryan and Maggie before speed-walking toward the porta potties.

U

Tally closed herself inside a porta potty, sat down on the edge of the toilet seat, and sobbed. It was much easier to not think about Goose when he wasn't right in front of her. She cried for the pony she missed. She cried because he couldn't be hers. And she cried because, as long as she was a catch rider, she'd have to keep saying goodbye to animals she loved, only seeing them with their happy new owners.

"You okay, hon?" a voice from the next stall asked.

"I'm fine," Tally said, steadying her voice. "Thank you."

Tally let herself cry a little longer and then pulled it together. Relieved that she'd worn sunglasses, Tally pulled them down over her eyes and walked back out to the Dover ring.

She got back just in time to see Maggie at the in-gate, just a pony or two away from her A-show debut. Tally could practically feel her anxiety. Lupe used a rag to shine Maggie's boots and another rag to wipe Joey's mouth before they went in.

"You'll be great," Tally told her. Maggie let out a big breath.

"Why am I so nervous?"

"I'm nervous every time," Tally said. "Until we get over the first jump. Then it's more fun."

"Okay, Mags, you ready?" Ryan asked, his arm draped over Joey's rump.

"Green single, judge's line in six, diagonal seven, outside six, single oxer," Maggie recited.

"You got it. Go have fun," he told her.

Maggie entered the ring and Ryan stepped up to the in-gate and crossed his arms—his usual in-gate pose, Tally noticed.

Maggie was a little slow to the first jump. "Come on, come on, stop pulling," Tally heard Ryan say softly. "Pick it up," he said a little louder as Maggie approached the in-gate before turning toward the judge's line. "Relax your elbows and let him canter on."

Maggie and Joey jumped the judge's line much better than the first jump and by the time they turned for the diagonal line, Joey was fully in show mode, flowing down the seven strides. They turned for the last line.

"Good, Maggie, just keep that canter," Ryan said as they passed by again.

They jumped the outside line well and turned for the final oxer. It was a bit of a chip, but nothing terrible, and when they cantered their closing circle, you could see Maggie's smile from two rings over.

"Maggie, great!" Ryan said as they walked out of the ring. "I think you got excited to get to that last jump and you cut the turn a little." Maggie nodded, still smiling. "That's why you went past the distance there—because cutting your turn changed the track. Are you with me? But really good job for your first show on a new pony."

Tally put her hand up to give Maggie a high five.

"It wasn't fun until, like, the third or fourth jump," Maggie said with a laugh.

"My pony didn't even get *over* one jump at my first A show," Tally said with a laugh. "You're doing great."

Maggie's second course was better than the first, and her third course was the best of all. Tally didn't think she stopped smiling all the way through their under saddle. And when the announcer called out the placings, Maggie and Joey got great ribbons, ending up reserve champion of the division.

CHAPTER 22

After Maggie was done and the next division got started with their jumping classes, Tally put her vest on over her show coat. At home, zipping up her vest had become as normal as putting on her helmet—just another piece of equipment that she wore whenever she rode. And Ryan had been right about the heat. She did get used to it after a week or two, no longer feeling like she was in an oven while riding. When she rode Obie in the schooling ring, she'd put the vest on over her show shirt, and it was no big deal. But putting it on over her show coat was different.

For starters, Tally felt like the sleeves of her coat bunched up at the shoulders underneath the vest. She no longer had the clean, crisp look she loved when she put on her show clothes. And Tally didn't see anyone else on the showgrounds in a vest. She'd only been at the stalls, the Dover ring, and the warm-up area just outside it. But if anyone in those areas had a vest on, Tally definitely would have noticed. It was just her.

"You ready to get on?" Ryan asked, interrupting Tally's thoughts.

"Yup."

"What's up? You look distracted." Nothing ever got past Ryan.

"Do you think the judge will notice my vest?" Tally asked, her voice softer than she'd intended. Ryan looked thoughtful.

"Maybe. But it has nothing to do with your performance or Obie's," he told her.

"I know, but…I'm the only one here wearing a vest."

"Not true," Ryan said firmly. "I saw at least a couple in the junior hunters yesterday."

"Really?"

Ryan nodded. "And even if you *were* the only one, you made a decision to take safety seriously. It's allowed in the rule book, and no judge will hold it against you."

Tally exhaled, feeling herself physically relax. She thanked Ryan and mounted up, noticing that Obie stood just as still at the horse show mounting block as he did at home.

Entering the ring for their warm-up hack class, Tally could feel that Obie wanted to stare at the colorful judge's line. When he didn't respond to her leg, Tally used a little spur and put a slight inside bend on him. Obie flicked an ear back at her and stepped into a trot. He opened up a bit in front of the judge. Was Obie showing off?

Throughout the under saddle, Tally could feel Obie staring at various things in the ring, but she would whisper the word "confident" to herself and just keep adding leg. It seemed like Obie trusted her and felt the confidence, and he didn't fully spook or balk at anything.

U

"Line up in the center of the ring with your numbers facing the judge," said the announcer. Tally had never cared about a ribbon less. It was just so cool to have brought Obie into a new situation and given him a positive experience.

The announcer rattled off first through third place. "Fourth place," he continued, "goes to Oceanfront and Tally Hart." Tally was pleasantly surprised to hear Obie's name called early in a big hack class and happily collected her ribbon.

Ryan had put her in the first group for the over fences classes so Tally watched the rider before her and thought about how she'd handle it if Obie balked at any of the jumps.

"I think you should trot the first jump no matter what," Ryan said. "This is an unrated division and trotting isn't penalized. If everyone else canters, so what? We're here to give Obie a positive first show experience. Sound good?"

Tally nodded.

"Okay, you're up. Have fun."

Tally squeezed Obie and they walked into the ring. Now that they were in there alone, rather than with a bunch of other horses for the hack, Obie felt a little less brave.

"Confident," Tally whispered. She almost asked Obie to canter out of habit on their way to the green single. Tally took a deep breath and reminded herself of her objective: Get over all eight jumps and give her horse confidence. Trot the first jump and then just play it by ear.

They trotted to the base of the green vertical and Obie gave it a round, lofty effort. They cantered away and Tally let out a big sigh of relief. *Jump one: done.*

Tally didn't think about much more than *leg* for the rest of the course. They trotted some jumps and cantered the outs of the lines when Obie felt brave and forward. Ryan looked happy when they exited the ring.

"Really good work, Tally," he said. "If you feel like you can canter more of the jumps in the next trips, go for it. But if he's forward, straight, and trotting, that's fine, too. We're not going for perfect here. Just eight jumps and a positive ride."

Two more times, Tally accomplished exactly that. Her second course was probably the best, cantering all of the jumps and only trotting for the simple changes. By the end of the third course, both she and Obie were tired and he broke to the trot before one of the lines, so they added. He nearly broke to the trot again when they were cantering in the final hack class, but Tally was able to squeeze enough canter out of him for another fourth-place hack ribbon.

"Well done, Tal, you gave this guy a great first horse show," Ryan said as he picked up Tally's hack ribbon and gave Obie a pat. "I hope you're proud of yourself. *I'm* proud of you! Oh, and did you see who's here?"

Tally glanced around. Her parents usually made themselves scarce at shows so as not to make Tally nervous. "No, who?"

"Look behind you," said Ryan.

CHAPTER 23

"Mac! What are you doing here?" Tally was so happy to see her friend, she didn't even care that her shouting brought on stares from many of the people standing around them.

Tally halted Obie and Mac grinned and caught up to them.

"I came to cheer you on," Mac said, a bit of shyness in her voice. "Congratulations. Obie looked great."

"Thanks," Tally said. "I've missed you so much."

"Me too," Mac said. They walked together in silence back to the stalls, where Tally untacked Obie and put on his shipping halter. Lupe asked if he could give Obie a bath for her.

"Could I hand graze him first?" Tally asked. "Bath after?"

Lupe gave her two thumbs up. Tally, Obie, and Mac strolled up a small hill past the warm-up ring to a grassy open field.

"Thanks again for the bracelet," Mac said, looking at the ground while absentmindedly rubbing Obie's shoulder. "And for your note. That was really nice of you."

"I meant everything I wrote," Tally replied, sounding a bit shy and awkward herself.

"I'm sorry I ghosted you, I just..." Mac was still looking down as she gathered her thoughts. "What you said brought back a lot of hurt feelings from my old barn. I felt like every-one there thought they were better than me. I mean, they did feel that way. I'd hear them talking about it."

"I didn't think that at all," Tally began, but Mac held her hand up.

"I know you didn't," Mac told her. Her expression landed somewhere between sad and apologetic. "It's been really hard not riding since I broke my wrist. I feel like I've spent the past month just feeling sorry for myself. You got on Joey and everything just seemed so easy for you."

Tally nodded.

"But then I rode him the other day and things came right back. For the most part...I mean, my legs hurt for a full two days afterward," Mac said with a laugh. Then her face turned serious again. "I rode with a bunch of mean girls at my old barn. I would literally hear them saying I couldn't ride and that's why I was always falling off my old pony. It was awful and it went on for such a long time. I don't think you're like that at all, and it's not your fault. It just brought back those memories."

"That makes sense," Tally said. Obie picked his head up to stare at something in the distance. Then he stuck his muzzle back down into the grass.

"I'm glad you know I didn't mean it like that at all," Tally added.

Mac nodded. "I was a bad friend for ignoring you. I'm sorry, Tal."

♘

Tally wrapped her friend up in a hug. "It's okay!" she said. "But it's really not that easy for me, just so you know. Riding is never easy and neither is being a catch rider. I saw Goose this morning and I had to run away and bawl in the porta potties."

"I don't blame you! He was so sweet. You'll have your own horse one day, Tally, I'm sure of it. And until then, you get a lot of great rides."

"That is true," Tally said, a smile spreading across her face.

The girls walked Obie back to the wash stall and Ryan intercepted them.

"Your ribbons, Tal," he said, waving a pile of white and pink rosettes and placing them on top of her tack trunk. There might have been a peek of yellow in there, too.

"Ryan, will you take a picture?" Mac asked, handing Ryan her phone.

"Say 'horse shows!'" said Ryan.

"Horse shows!" the girls said in unison.

Mac took the phone back from Ryan and flipped it around to show Tally the picture. Tally's face was red in the photo, and her vest definitely wasn't as beautiful as her show coat was by itself, but Tally didn't mind either one. She hoped the shot would make the photo collage in the tack room back home.

"Want to look up what you got in each class?" Mac asked. Tally shook her head no. She'd figure that out later, just in order to write the notes on the backs of her ribbons—her little tradition so she could look back at them later and see the progress she'd made with showing.

Tally never heard the placings announced, and for the first time, it wasn't the highlight of her show day. She had good rides on her horse, and, even better, she had her best friend back.

That was winning.

Catch up on the
***SHOW STRIDES* series!**

School Horses and Show Ponies

Confidence Comeback

Moving Up and Moving On

Always available at
theplaidhorse.com

ABOUT THE AUTHORS

Piper Klemm, Ph.D. is the publisher of *The Plaid Horse* magazine. She co-hosts the weekly podcast of The Plaid Horse, the #Plaidcast, and is a college professor. She has been riding since she was eight years old and currently owns several hunter ponies who compete on the horse show circuit. She frequently competes in the Adult Amateurs across North America on her horse of a lifetime MTM Sandwich, so you might see her at a horse show near you!

FIND HER ONLINE AT piper-klemm.com
🄾 **@piperklemm**

Rennie Dyball has loved horses ever since she was a little girl. She began taking lessons at age twelve, competed with the Penn State equestrian team, and, after a long riding hiatus while building her career in New York City, she's back to showing in the hunter ring. Rennie spent fifteen years as a writer and editor at *People* magazine and People.com, has co-authored a dozen books, and her picture book debut will be published in 2023. With *Show Strides*, Rennie is delighted to combine two of her greatest passions—writing and riding.

FIND HER ONLINE AT renniedyball.com
🄾 **@renniedyball**
🐦 **@renniedyball**

WHO'S WHO
AT QUINCE OAKS

Ava Foster: Friends with Tally and Kaitlyn, used to own Danny but quit riding to pursue gymnastics

Beau: Field Ridge pony who belongs to a rider named Marion

Brenna: Barn manager at Quince Oaks

Carlo: Jacob's horse, a jumper

Cindy Bennett: Mac's mom

Field Ridge: Ryan's business within Quince Oaks

Gelati: A school pony at Quince Oaks

Goose: A green small pony that Tally catch-rode

Isabelle: A teenage junior rider who trains with Ryan

Jacob Viston: A junior rider who trains with Ryan

James Hart: Tally's dad

Jordan: Takes lessons at Quince Oaks, sometimes with Tally

Kaitlyn Rowe: Tally's best friend at school

Kelsey: Working student for the riding school

Little Bit: A school pony at Quince Oaks

Lupe: Field Ridge's head groom

Mackenzie (Mac) Bennett: Junior rider who owns Joey

Maggie Edwards: Junior rider who trains with Ryan

Marsha: The barn secretary at Quince Oaks

Meg: Tally's instructor at Quince Oaks before Ryan

Obie: Tally's project horse

Olivia Motes: A rider who bought Goose after trying him at Pony Finals

Pip: Isabelle's junior hunter

Quince Oaks: The barn

Ryan McNeil: The Field Ridge trainer who operates out of Quince Oaks

Scout: One of the Quince Oaks school horses

Smoke Hill Jet Set (Joey at the barn): Mac's medium pony hunter

Stacy Hart: Tally's mom

Stonelea Dance Party (Danny at the barn): Formerly Ava Foster's pony, sold through Ryan

Sweet Talker (Sweetie at the barn): Tally's favorite school horse

Tally (Natalia) Hart: Rides in the lesson program and Ryan's sales ponies at Quince Oaks

GLOSSARY OF HORSE TERMINOLOGY

A circuit: Nationally-rated horse shows.

backed: When a horse or pony that's newly in training has a rider on its back for the first time.

base: Where a horse or pony leaves the ground in front of a jump; also: refers to the rider's feet in the stirrups, with heels down acting as anchors, or a base of support, for the rider's legs.

bay: A horse color that consists of a brown coat and black points (black mane, tail, ear edges, and legs).

buzzer: The sound in the jumper ring that indicates a horse and rider have forty-five seconds to cross the timers in front of the first jump.

canter: A three-beat gait that horses and ponies travel in—it's a more controlled version of the gallop, the fastest of the gaits (walk, trot, canter, gallop).

catch-riding: When a rider gets to ride and/or show a horse or pony for someone else.

cavaletti: Very small jumps for schooling or jumping practice.

chestnut: A reddish brown horse/pony coat color, with a lighter mane and tail.

chip: When a horse or pony takes off too close to a jump by adding in an extra stride near the base.

colic: A catch-all term for gastrointestinal distress in a horse or pony; can be fatal in severe cases.

colt: A young male horse.

conformation class: A horse show class in which the animals are modeled and judged on their build.

crest release: When the rider places his or her hands up the horse or pony's neck, thus adding slack to the reins and giving the animal freedom of movement in its head and neck.

crop/bat: A small (and humane!) whip that is used behind the rider's leg when the rider's leg aid is not sufficient.

cross-rail: A jump consisting of two rails in the shape of an X.

currycomb: A grooming tool used in circles on a horse or pony's coat to lift out dirt.

Devon: An annual, prestigious invitation-only horse show in Pennsylvania.

diagonal line: Two jumps with a set distance between them set on the diagonal of a riding ring.

distance: The take-off spot for a jump. Riders often talk about "finding distances," which means finding the ideal spot to take off over a jump.

flower boxes: Like "walls," these are jump adornments that are placed below the lowest rail of a jump.

gate: Part of a jump that is placed in the jump cups instead of a rail. Typically heavier than a standard jump rail so horses and ponies can be more careful in jumping them so as not to hit a hoof.

gelding: A castrated male horse.

girth: A piece of equipment that holds the saddle securely on a horse or pony. The girth attaches to the billets under the flaps of the saddle and goes underneath the horse, behind the front legs, and is secured on the billets on the other side.

green: A horse or pony who has less training and/or experience (the opposite of a "made" horse or pony, which has lots of training and experience).

gymnastic: A line of jumps with one, two, or zero strides between them (no strides in between jumps is called a bounce—the horse or pony lands off the first jump and immediately takes off for the next without taking a stride).

hack: Can either mean riding a horse on the flat (no jumps) in an indoor ring or outside; or, an under saddle class at a horse show, in which the animal is judged on its performance on the flat.

hands: A unit of measurement for horse or pony heights. One hand equals 4 inches, so a 15-hand horse is 60 inches tall from the ground to its withers. A pony that's 12.2 hands is 12 hands, 2 inches, or 50 inches tall at the withers.

handy: A handy class in a hunter division is meant to test a horse or pony's handiness, or its ability to navigate a course. Special elements included in handy hunter courses may include trot jumps, roll backs, and hand gallops.

in-and-out: Two jumps with one stride in between, typically part of a jumper or equitation course.

in-gate: Sometimes just referred to as "the gate," it's where horses enter and exit the show ring. Usually it's one gate for both directions; sometimes two gates will be in use, one to go in and the other to come out.

jog: How ponies and horses in A-rated divisions finish each over fences class; the judge calls them to jog across the ring to check for soundness and orders the class. During the COVID-19 pandemic, the closing circle trot was used in place of the jog.

jump-off: An element in many jumper classes in which horses and riders jump a shortened course, and the fastest time with the fewest jumping and time faults wins.

large pony: A pony that measures over 13.2 hands, but no taller than 14.2 hands.

lead changes: Changing of the canter lead from right to left or vice versa. The inside front and hind legs stretch farther when the horse or pony is on the correct lead. A lead change can be executed in two ways: A simple lead change is when the horse transitions from the canter to the trot and then picks up the opposite canter lead. In a flying lead change, the horse changes their lead in midair without trotting.

line: Two jumps with a set number of strides between them.

longe line: A long lead that attaches to a horse's halter or bridle. The horse or pony travels around the handler in a large circle to work on the flat with commands from the handler holding the line.

Maclay: One of the big equitation or "big eq" classes for junior riders. Riders compete in regional Maclay classes to qualify for the annual Maclay Final. The final is currently held at the National Horse Show at the Kentucky Horse Park in the fall.

mare: A mature female horse.

martingale: A piece of tack intended to keep a horse or pony from raising its head too high. The martingale attaches to the girth, between the animal's front legs, and then (in a standing martingale) a single strap attaches to the noseband or (in a running martingale) a pair of straps attach to the reins.

medium pony: A pony taller than 12.2 hands, but no taller than 13.2 hands.

outside line: A line of jumps with a set number of strides between them set on the long sides of the riding ring. An outside line set on the same side of the ring as the judge's box/stand is called a judge's line.

oxer: A type of jump that features two sets of standards and two top rails, which can be set even (called a square oxer) or uneven, with the back rail higher than the front. A typical hunter over fences class features single oxers as well as oxers set as the "out" jump in lines.

palomino: A horse or pony with a golden color coat and a white mane and tail.

pinned: The way a horse show class is ordered and ribbons are awarded, typically from first through sixth or first through eighth place (though some classes go to tenth or even twentieth place).

polos: Also called polo wraps, they provide protection and support to a horse or pony's legs while being ridden.

pommel: The front part of an English saddle; the rider sits behind this.

Pony Finals: An annual show, currently held at the Kentucky Horse Park, in which ponies who were champion or reserve at an A-rated show are eligible to compete.

posting trot: When a rider posts (stands up and sits down in the saddle) as the horse or pony is trotting, making the gait more comfortable and less bouncy for both the rider and the animal.

quarter sheet: A blanket intended for cold weather riding that attaches under the saddle flaps and loops under the horse or pony's tail.

regular pony hunter division (sometimes called "the division"): A national or A-rated horse show division in which small ponies jump 2'3", medium ponies jump 2'6", and large ponies jump 2'9"–3'.

rein: The reins are part of the bridle and attach to the horse or pony's bit. Used for steering and slowing down.

sales pony/sales horse: A pony or horse that is offered for sale; trainers often market a sales horse or pony through ads and by showing the animal.

school horses/school ponies: Horses or ponies who are used in a program teaching riding lessons.

schooling ring: A ring at a horse show designated for warming up or schooling.

schooling shows: Unrated shows intended for practice as well as for green horses and ponies to gain experience.

shadbelly: A formal show coat with tails typically worn for hunter classics and derbies.

small pony: A pony that measures 12.2 hands and under.

spooky: A horse or pony that's acting easily spooked or startled.

spurs: An artificial aid, worn on a rider's boots to add impulsion.

stakes class: Part of a hunter division; it's a class that offers prize money.

stirrup irons: The metal loops in which riders place their feet.

stirrup leathers: Threaded through the stirrup bars of the saddle and through the stirrups themselves; the leathers hold the stirrups in place.

swap: When a horse or pony unnecessarily changes its lead on course.

tack: The equipment a horse wears to be ridden (e.g. saddle, bridle, martingale).

tall boots: The knee-high, black leather boots that hunter/jumper/equitation riders wear with breeches when they reach a certain height or age. Prior to that, riders wear paddock boots (which only reach past the ankles) and jodhpurs with garter straps.

ticketed schooling: Opportunities offered by some horse shows to ride in show rings unjudged, as practice for horses and riders.

trail rides: A ride that takes places out on trails instead of in a riding ring.

transition: When a horse or pony moves from one gait to another. For example, moving from the canter to the trot is a downward transition; moving from the walk to the trot is an upward transition.

trot: A two-beat gait in which the horse or pony's legs move in diagonal pairs.

tricolors: The ribbons awarded for champion (most points in a division) and reserve champion (second highest number of points in that division).

trip: Another term for a jumping round, or course, mostly used at shows, as in, "the pony's first trip."

vertical: A jump that includes one set of standards and a rail or rails set horizontally.

THE PLAID HORSE

ENCOURAGES EVERY YOUNG EQUESTRIAN TO:

READ   *The Plaid Horse* magazine
In print and online at
theplaidhorse.com/read

Subscribe at **theplaidhorse.com/subscribe**

READ   The re-release of
Geoff Teall on Riding Hunters, Jumpers and Equitation: Develop a Winning Style

Available at **theplaidhorse.com/books**

READ   *The Plaid Horse*'s forthcoming
With Purpose: The Balmoral Standard
by Carleton Brooks and Traci Brooks

Available at **theplaidhorse.com/books**

LISTEN   The #Plaidcast
The podcast of The Plaid Horse at
theplaidhorse.com/listen

On Horse Radio Network, Audible, Apple Podcasts, Google Play, Stitcher, and Spotify

LEARN   Explore your college credit education opportunities at **theplaidhorse.com/college**

WEAR   Find your apparel style at **plaidhorsestore.com**

ENGAGE   Find out about local events featuring Piper & Rennie at **theplaidhorse.com**

FOLLOW   The Plaid Horse on social media:

- Facebook.com/theplaidhorsemag
- Twitter @PlaidHorsemag
- Instagram @theplaidhorsemag
- Pinterest @theplaidhorsemag

GEOFF TEALL ON RIDING HUNTERS, JUMPERS AND EQUITATION: DEVELOP A WINNING STYLE

Recently re-released, this guide by top trainer Geoff Teall details how to increase the effectiveness of the time you spend in the saddle, whether you are a beginning hunt seat rider or a seasoned competitor.

EXCERPTED BELOW: Piper Klemm's introduction from the book

Note to the reader: Growing up as a horse enthusiast, I checked out every single book about horses from my local library—most of them many times. I read every second that I couldn't be actually at the barn learning horsemanship hands-on. My own riding career had its ups and downs, my background consuming equine knowledge and my love of horses led me to eventually publishing *The Plaid Horse.*

When I started teaching college equestrian courses, I sat down with all of the resources our market had to offer and was happily surprised by the wealth of information that has come out in the last twenty years. Upon reading and reflecting on all of these books, the standout text was clearly *Geoff Teall on Riding Hunters, Jumpers and Equitation.*

⚘

Geoff Teall on Riding Hunters, Jumpers, and Equitation is the fundamental primer that I hope every rider or aspiring rider takes the time to read thoroughly. And I hope they will re-read it every few years, applying their own enhanced experiences and perspectives to each reading. For the seasoned rider, it is such a thoughtful and clear take on the fundamentals, which often are sadly lost in our fast-paced and overly horse-show-centric environment. The book impressed me so much that *The Plaid Horse* wanted to be a part of its new life with a new printing in order to get it into as many equestrians' hands as possible. Geoff's work remains as strong and relevant as ever. As much as things have changed in our sport, so much about riding hunters, jumpers, and equitation does not. Classic still wins in the show ring.

Riders can take responsibility for so many aspects of this sport: their discipline, their preparation, the goals they are trying to achieve, and their mental game. Geoff goes through every facet of both technical riding and how to navigate the world of hunters, jumpers and equitation for the best results possible. He discusses listening to the horse; training and care in a no-frills, horse-centered mentality; and the steps each individual must take to have opportunities opened up to them. His discussions on getting help, undermounting yourself, and setting appropriate goals are frank, coherent, and straightforward.

Good fundamentals take so long to learn, but they are the only approach for long-term success in this industry. While gimmicks and shortcuts can seem to be all the rage, they always end up falling short, left in the dust over time by the earnings and winnings of true horse people. In this book and in person, Geoff evangelizes the horse's well-being and safety over winning, taking the time to train both horse and rider properly before competition, and putting a lifelong riding career over a single goal.

It's been a privilege to teach equestrian college courses and to help educate people in our sport through *The Plaid Horse*. Reminding riders how much they do have within their control in this sport is a prompting we all need, and Geoff's forthright discussions help people make better observations at every level.

In the pages that follow, Geoff clearly lays out how to grow your mastery of this sport and all it entails, from mental game, to appropriate goals, to enjoying your animals. We hope you enjoy reading this superb book.

—Piper Klemm

Publisher, *The Plaid Horse*
Professor of Sports Studies
Host of *The #Plaidcast*
Author of *Show Strides*

Look for
**SHOW STRIDES
BOOK 5**
in 2022!